The Fables
of
John Gay
Volume 1

*To Sarah
With Best Wishes
from Dandi*

The Fables of John Gay
Volume One

Illustrated by Dandi Palmer

First published by Tonson and Watts in 1727

This edition published by Dodo Books 2008

Illustrations © Dandi Palmer 2008

ISBN 978 1 906442 04 0

Typefaces:
Titles - Harrington
Text - 12pt Century Schoolbook

John Gay
dedicated these Fables to the infant
William, Duke of Cumberland,
second son of George II.

The illustrator of this edition would like
to add an appreciation for the
wit, words, and wisdom
of
Stephen Fry
and all those like minds who
have the same humour and
interest in the World.

CONTENTS

John Gay

Introduction - The Shepherd and the Philosopher

1 -- The Lion, the Tiger, and the Traveller
2 -- The Spaniel and the Chameleon
3 -- The Mother, the Nurse, and the Fairy
4 -- The Eagle and the Assembly of Animals
5 -- The Wild Boar and the Ram
6 -- The Miser and Plutus
7 -- The Lion, the Fox, and the Geese
8 -- The Lady and the Wasp
9 -- The Bull and the Mastiff
10 -- The Elephant and the Bookseller
11 -- The Peacock, the Turkey, and Goose
12 -- Cupid, Hymen, and Plutus
13 -- The Tame Stag
14 -- The Monkey Who had Seen the World
15 -- The Philosopher and the Pheasant
16 -- The Pin and Needle
17 -- The Shepherd's Dog and the Wolf
18 -- The Painter who Pleased Nobody and Everybody
19 -- The Lion and the Cub
20 -- The Old Hen and the Cock
21 -- The Rat-Catcher and Cats
22 -- The Goat Without a Beard
23 -- The Old Woman and Her Cats
24 -- The Butterfly and the Snail
25 -- The Scold and the Parrot

26 -- The Cur and the Mastiff
27 -- The Sick Man and the Angel
28 -- The Persian, the Sun, and the Cloud
29 -- The Fox at the Point of Death
30 -- The Setting-Dog and the Partridge
31 -- The Universal Apparition
32 -- The Two Owls and the Sparrow
33 -- The Courtier and Proteus
34 -- The Mastiff
35 -- The Barley-Mow and the Dunghill
36 -- Pythagoras and the Countryman
37 -- The Farmer's Wife and the Raven
38 -- The Turkey and the Ant
39 -- The Father and Jupiter
40 -- The Two Monkeys
41 -- The Owl and the Farmer
42 -- The Jugglers
43 -- The Council of Horses
44 -- The Hound and the Huntsman
45 -- The Poet and the Rose
46 -- The Cur, the Horse, and the Shepherd's Dog
47 -- The Court of Death
48 -- The Gardener and the Hog
49 -- The Man and the Flea
50 -- The Hare and Many Friends

John Gay

John Gay wrote a tragedy called 'The Captives', which was performed at Drury lane in January 1724. The Author also read it to the Princess of Wales. Impressed, she asked him to write some fables for her infant son, the Duke of Cumberland. In 1727, after some delay in the preparation of the illustrations and plates by John Wootton the animal painter and Kent, the architect, Tonson and Watts published Volume 1 of the Fables. The most noted edition of the Fables, with wood engravings by Thomas Bewick, appeared in 1779. Gay is now principally known as the author of 'The Beggar's Opera'. For some time his Fables had been just as popular, especially with the Victorians.

Gay completed a second volume of Fables in the year of his death in 1732 and they appeared in 1733. These poems are much longer and 'mostly on subjects of a graver and more political turn'.

John Gay was born in Barnstaple, Devon, and baptised on 16th, September 1685. He was the youngest child of William Gay and Katherine Hanmer. They also had an older son and two daughters, another daughter dying shortly before John's birth. The family were descended from the Le Gays of Oxford and Devonshire and, although not wealthy, were comfortably off. Gay's mother died in 1694 when he was only ten. His father died the next year. One of four paternal uncles took charge of the orphaned family. The elder brother, Jonathan, joined the army and rose to captain before dying in 1709 at the age of 31, and the two sisters, Catherine and Joanna, married.

After a grammar school education John Gay was apprenticed to a silk mercer in London. He gave up the vocation, or was dismissed, and returned to Barnstaple. He stayed with his mother's brother, the Rev. John Hanmer, a nonconformist minister, before returning to London. Some poems discovered in the minister's favourite chair a century later were attributed to Gay. Authorship is not certain and these seem to be the only work from that period of his youth. Though in London for some while, little is known about how Gay survived until the publication of his poem 'Wine' in 1703. The poet's friendly and compliant nature later earned for him such friends as Alexander Pope, Jonathan Swift and Dr. John Arbuthnot.

In 1712 Gay obtained the post of secretary to the Duchess of Monmouth, wife of Charles II's illegitimate son who had been beheaded for trying to overthrow James II. This eccentric and difficult employer dispensed with his services in 1714. In the middle of the year, owing to the influence of his friends, Gay was appointed secretary to Lord Clarendon who was about to visit the Court of Hanover. On payment of £100, Gay promptly used it to buy a sumptuous outfit to impress the German court. On the 1st, August Queen Anne died and Lord Clarendon and his secretary were recalled. Gay was once again left without a patron or employer.

From then on Gay willingly gave up his independence to become the protégé of anyone indulgent enough to support his indolent habits and liking for good food and wine.

By his own admission, Gay was fat and disliked exercise. It was probably the combination of the two that hastened his comparatively early death. Sooner than walk a short distance, he always made sure a coach was at his disposal when in London.

Gay could not cope wisely with penury or the sudden acquisition of wealth. Against all good advice, he invested the considerable fortune of £20,000 in South Sea stock. He lost it all when the bubble burst in 1720. Then came the success of his play, 'The Beggar's Opera' with music by Johann Pepusch. It was staged by John Rich at Lincoln's Inn Fields in 1723.

Its profits enabled Rich to build the first theatre in Covent Garden. Though not well remunerated, John Gay became famous, as well as notorious with those who claimed the play was immoral. The real profit came from 'Polly', its sequel. The Lord Chamberlain, under instruction from Sir Robert Walpole, prohibited its performance. As a consequence, printed copies of the text sold at a phenomenal rate. Given Gay's easy and eager to please nature, it is unlikely he courted infamy of any description. Even the scandalous play 'Three Hours After Marriage', though attributed to him, was jointly written by Pope and Arbuthnot as well.

Gay was able to use language in a fluid and natural way all levels of society understood. Many of his moral stands did vary in height, although he does consistently declare his abhorrence of butchers.

In 1723, Gay's health deteriorated severely. With the attention of Dr. Arbuthnot and the Duke and Duchess of Queensbury, his last patrons, he survived.

Gay died in 1732 at the town house in Burlington Gardens of the Duke and Duchess. According to Dr. Arbuthnot 'of an inflammation and I believe at last a mortification of the bowels.'

Due to the management of Gay's money by the Duke of Queensbury, the poet left £6,000. As Gay made no will and never married, the money and the proceeds from a theatrical benefit went to his widowed sisters, Catherine Baller and Joanna Fortescue.

The Duke and Duchess of Queensbury had a memorial erected to John Gay in Westminster Abbey where he was buried. It was in Poet's Corner until 1936 when it was removed with some others after the discovery of two medieval paintings of St. Christopher and St. Thomas behind the wall they stood against. It is now in the Triforium, unfortunately out of the public view.

Alexander Pope's lines on the monument give an idea of Gay's character from someone who knew him well:-

> Of Manners gentle, of Affections mild;
> In Wit a Man; Simplicity a child:
> With native Humour temp'ring virtuous Rage,
> Form'd to delight at once and lash the Age:
> Above Temptation, in a low Estate,
> And uncorrupted, ev'n among the Great;
> A safe Companion, and an easy Friend,
> Unblam'd thro' Life, lamented in thy End.
> These are thy Honours: not that here thy Bust.
> Is mix'd with Heroes, or with Kings thy Dust;
> But the Worthy and the Good shall say,
> Striking their pensive bosoms _ Here lies GAY.

Gay's two line epitaph to himself probably says more about the poet and playwright:-

> Life is a jest; and all things show it,
> I thought so once: but now I know it.

Jane Palmer 1984

The illustrator wishes to thank the following:
The National Galleries of Scotland, who own the portrait of John Gay by William Aikman from which the title page illustration was taken;
The Dean and Chapter of Westminster for supplying the photograph of John Gay's memorial and other information, both of which were invaluable;
The Guildhall Library, who own the original picture of Gresham College in Bishopsgate Street, from which the illustration of Fable 16, 'The Pin and the Needle' was copied.

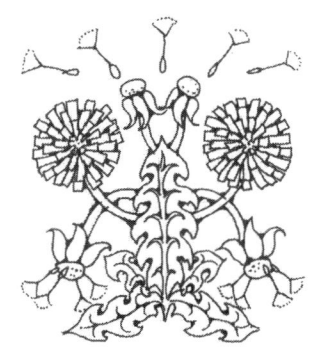

Other Works by John Gay

Wine	1708
The Mohocks	1712
The Present State of Wit	1711
Rural Sports	1713
The Wife of Bath	1713
The Shepherd's Week	1714
The What D'Ye Call It	1715
Trivia, or The Art of Walking the Streets of London	1716
Three Hours After Marriage	1717
The Captives	1724
Fables, Volume One	1727
The Beggar's Opera	1728
Polly	1729
Acis and Galatea	1732
Fables, Volume Two	1733
Achilles	1733
The Distress'd Wife	1734

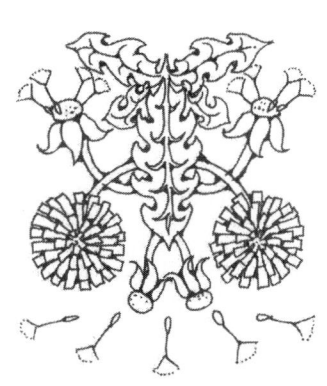

INTRODUCTION

The Shepherd and the Philosopher

Remote from cities lived a Swain,
Unvex'd with all the cares of gain;
His head was silver'd o'er with age,
And long experience made him sage;
In summer's heat and winter's cold
He fed his flock and penn'd the fold:
His hours in cheerful labour flew,
Nor envy nor ambition knew:
His wisdom and his honest fame
Through all the country raised his name.
  A deep Philosopher (whose rules
Of moral life were drawn from schools)
The Shepherd's homely cottage sought,
And thus explored his reach of thought:
  "Whence is thy learning? Hath thy toil
O'er books consumed the midnight oil?
Hast thou old Greece and Rome survey'd,
And the vast sense of Plato weigh'd?
Hath Socrates thy soul refined,
And hast thou fathom'd Tully's mind?
Or, like the wise Ulysses, thrown,
By various fates, on realms unknown,
Hast thou through many cities stray'd,
Their customs, laws, and manners weigh'd ?"
The Shepherd modestly replied,
"I ne'er the paths of learning tried;
Nor have I roam'd in foreign parts
To read mankind, their laws and arts;
For man is practised in disguise,
He cheats the most discerning eyes:
Who by that search shall wiser grow,
When we ourselves can never know?
The little knowledge I have gain'd,

Was all from simple Nature drain'd;
Hence my life's maxims took their rise,
Hence grew my settled hate to vice.
The daily labours of the bee
Awake my soul to industry.
Who can observe the careful ant
And not provide for future want?
My dog (the trustiest of his kind)
With gratitude inflames my mind:
I mark his true, his faithful way,
And in my service copy Tray.
In constancy and nuptial love,
I learn my duty from the dove.
The hen, who from the chilly air,
With pious wing, protects her care,
And every fowl that flies at large
Instructs me in a parent's charge.
   "From Nature, too I take my rule,
To shun contempt and ridicule.
I never, with important air,
In conversation overbear.
Can grave and formal pass for wise,
When men the solemn owl despise?
My tongue within my lips I rein,
For who talks much, must talk in vain.
We from the wordy torrent fly:
Who listens to the chatt'ring pie?
Nor would I, with felonious sleight,
By stealth invade my neighbour's right.
Rapacious animals we hate:
Kites, hawks, and wolves, deserve their fate.
Do not we just abhorrence find
Against the toad and serpent kind?
But Envy, Calumny, and Spite,
Bear stronger venom in their bite.
Thus every object of creation
Can furnish hints to contemplation,
And from the most minute and mean,
A virtuous mind can morals glean."
   "Thy fame is just," the Sage replies,
"Thy virtue proves thee truly wise.
Pride often guides the author's pen:
Books as affected are as men:
But he who studies Nature's laws,
From certain truth his maxims draws;
And those, without our schools, suffice
To make men moral, good, and wise."

FABLE I

The Lion, the Tiger, and the Traveller

Accept, young Prince! the moral lay,
And in these Tales mankind survey;
With early virtues plant your breast,
The specious arts of vice detest.
Princes, like beauties, from their youth,
Are strangers to the voice of Truth;
Learn to contemn all praise betimes,
For flattery's the nurse of crimes;
Friendship by sweet reproof is shown,
(A virtue never near a throne;)
In courts such freedom must offend,
There, none presumes to be a friend.

To those of your exalted station,
Each courtier is a dedication.
Must I, too, flatter like the rest,
And turn my morals to a jest?
The Muse disdains to steal from those
Who thrive in courts by fulsome prose.
   But shall I hide your real praise,
Or tell you what a nation says?
They in your infant bosom trace
The virtues of your royal race;
In the fair dawning of your mind
Discern you generous, mild, and kind;
They see you grieve to hear distress,
And pant already to redress.
Go on, the height of good attain,
Nor let a nation hope in vain:
For hence we justly may presage
The virtues of a riper age.
True courage shall your bosom fire,
And future actions own your sire.
Cowards are cruel, but the brave
Love mercy, and delight to save.

A Tiger, roaming for his prey,
Sprung on a Traveller in the way;
The prostrate game a Lion spies,
And on the greedy tyrant flies:
With mingled roar resounds the wood,
Their teeth, their claws, distil with blood,
Till, vanquish'd by the Lion's strength,
The spotted foe extends his length.
The Man besought the shaggy lord,
And on his knees for life implored:
His life the generous hero gave.
Together walking to his cave,
The Lion thus bespoke his guest:
  "What hardy beast shall dare contest
My matchless strength? you saw the fight,
And must attest my power and right.
Forced to forego their native home,
My starving slaves at distance roam.
Within these woods I reign alone,
The boundless forest is my own.

Bears, wolves, and all the savage brood
Have dyed the regal den with blood.
These carcases on either hand,
Those bones that whiten all the land,
My former deeds and triumphs tell,
Beneath these jaws what numbers fell."
  "True," says the man, "the strength I saw
Might well the brutal nation awe:
But shall a monarch, brave, like you,
Place glory in so false a view?
Robbers invade their neighbour's right:
Be loved: let justice bound your might.
Mean are ambitious heroes' boasts
Of wasted lands, and slaughter'd hosts
Pirates their power by murders gain
Wise kings by love and mercy reign.
To me your clemency hath shown
The virtue worthy of a throne.
Heav'n gives you power above the rest,
Like Heav'n, to succour the distrest."
  "The case is plain," the Monarch said,
"False glory hath my youth misled;
For beasts of prey, a servile train,
Have been the flatterers of my reign.
You reason well. Yet tell me, friend,
Did ever you in courts attend?
For all my fawning rogues agree
That human heroes rule like me."

FABLE 2

The Spaniel and the Chameleon

A Spaniel, bred with all the care
That waits upon a favourite heir,
Ne'er felt correction's rigid hand;
Indulged to disobey command,
In pamper'd ease his hours were spent;
He never knew what learning meant.
Such forward airs, so pert, so smart,
Were sure to win his lady's heart;
Each little mischief gain'd him praise.
How pretty were his fawning ways!
   The wind was south, the morning fair,
He ventures forth to take the air.
He ranges all the meadow round,
And rolls upon the softest ground;
When near him a Chameleon seen,
Was scarce distinguish'd from the green.

"Dear emblem of the flattering host!
What, live with clowns! a genius lost!
To cities and the court repair;
A fortune cannot fail thee there:
Preferment shall thy talents crown;
Believe me, friend; I know the town."
  "Sir," says the Sycophant, "like you,
Of old, politer life I knew;
Like you, a courtier born and bred,
Kings lean'd their ear to what I said:
My whisper always met success;
The ladies praised me for address.
I knew to hit each courtier's passion,
And flattered every vice in fashion;
But Jove, who hates the liar's ways,
At once cut short my prosp'rous days,
And, sentenced to retain my nature,
Transform'd me to this crawling creature.
Doom'd to a life obscure and mean,
I wander in the sylvan scene:
For Jove the heart alone regards;
He punishes what man rewards.
How different is thy case and mine?
With men at least you sup and dine;
While I, condemn'd to thinnest fare,
Like those I flatter'd, feed on air."

FABLE 3

The Mother, the Nurse, and the Fairy

"Give me a son!" The blessing sent,
Were ever parents more content?
How partial are their doting eyes?
No child is half so fair and wise.
  Wak'd to the morning's pleasing care,
The Mother rose, and sought her heir:
She saw the Nurse like one possessed,
With wringing hands and sobbing breast;
  "Sure some disaster has befell:
Speak, Nurse; I hope the boy is well."
  "Dear Madam, think not me to blame,
Invisible the Fairy came:
Your precious babe is hence convey'd,
And in the place a changeling laid.
Where are the father's mouth and nose?
The mother's eyes, as black as sloes?
See, here, a shocking awkward creature,
That speaks a fool in every feature."

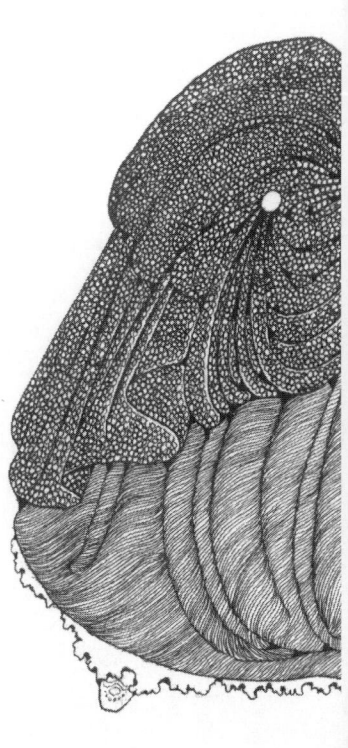

"The woman's blind," the Mother cries,
"I see wit sparkle in his eyes."
　"Lord, Madam, what a squinting leer!
No doubt the Fairy hath been here."
　Just as she spoke, a pigmy sprite
Pops through the keyhole swift as light;
Perch'd on the cradle's top he stands,
And thus her folly reprimands.
　"Whence sprung the vain conceited lie,
That we the world with fools supply?
What: give our sprightly race away
For the dull helpless sons of clay:
Besides, by partial fondness shown,
Like you, we dote upon our own.
Where yet was ever found a Mother,
Who'd give her booby for another?
And should we change for human breed,
Well might we pass for fools indeed."

FABLE 4

The Eagle and the Assembly of Animals

As Jupiter's all-seeing eye
Survey'd the worlds beneath the sky,
From this small speck of earth were sent
Murmurs and sounds of discontent;
For everything alive complain'd,
That he the hardest life sustain'd.
Jove calls his eagle. At the word
Before him stands the royal bird.
The bird, obedient, from heaven's height,
Downward directs his rapid flight;
Then cited every living thing
To hear the mandates of his king.
  "Ungrateful creatures! whence arise
These murmurs which offend the skies;
Why this disorder? say the cause;
For just are Jove's eternal laws.
Let each his discontent reveal:
To yon sour Dog I first appeal."
  "Hard is my lot," the Hound replies,
"On what fleet nerves the Greyhound flies;
While I, with weary step and slow,
O'er plains, and vales, and mountains go.
The morning sees my chase begun,
Nor ends it till the setting sun."

"When," says the Greyhound, "I pursue,
My game is lost, or caught in view;
Beyond my sight the prey's secure;
The hound is slow, but always sure;
And had I his sagacious scent,
Jove ne'er had heard my discontent."
  The Lion craved the Fox's art;
The Fox the Lion's force and heart:
The Cock implored the Pigeon's flight,
Whose wings were rapid, strong, and light;
The Pigeon strength of wing despised,
And the Cock's matchless valour prized:
The Fishes wished to graze the plain,
The Beasts to skim beneath the main:
Thus, envious of another's state,
Each blamed the partial hand of Fate.
  The Bird of Heaven then cried aloud
"Jove bids disperse the murmuring crowd;
The God rejects your idle prayers.
Would ye, rebellious mutineers!
Entirely change your name and nature,
And be the very envied creature?
What, silent all, and none consent?
Be happy then, and learn content;
Nor imitate the restless mind,
And proud ambition of mankind."

FABLE 5

The Wild Boar and the Ram

Against an elm a sheep was tied,
The butcher's knife in blood was dyed;
The patient flock, in silent fright,
From far beheld the horrid sight:
A savage Boar, who near them stood,
Thus mock'd to scorn the fleecy brood.
 "All cowards should be served like you.
See, see, your murd'rer is in view:
With purple hands, and reeking knife,
He strips the skin yet warm with life.
Your quarter'd sires, your bleeding dams,
The dying bleat of harmless lambs,
Call for revenge. O stupid race!
The heart that wants revenge is base."
 "I grant," an ancient Ram replies,
"We bear no terror in our eyes;
Yet think us not of soul so tame,
Which no repeated wrongs inflame;
Insensible of every ill,
Because we want thy tusks to kill.
Know, those who violence pursue,
Give to themselves the vengeance due;
For in these massacres they find
The two chief plagues that waste mankind
Our skin supplies the wrangling bar,
It wakes their slumbering sons to war;
And well revenge may rest contented,
Since drums and parchment were invented."

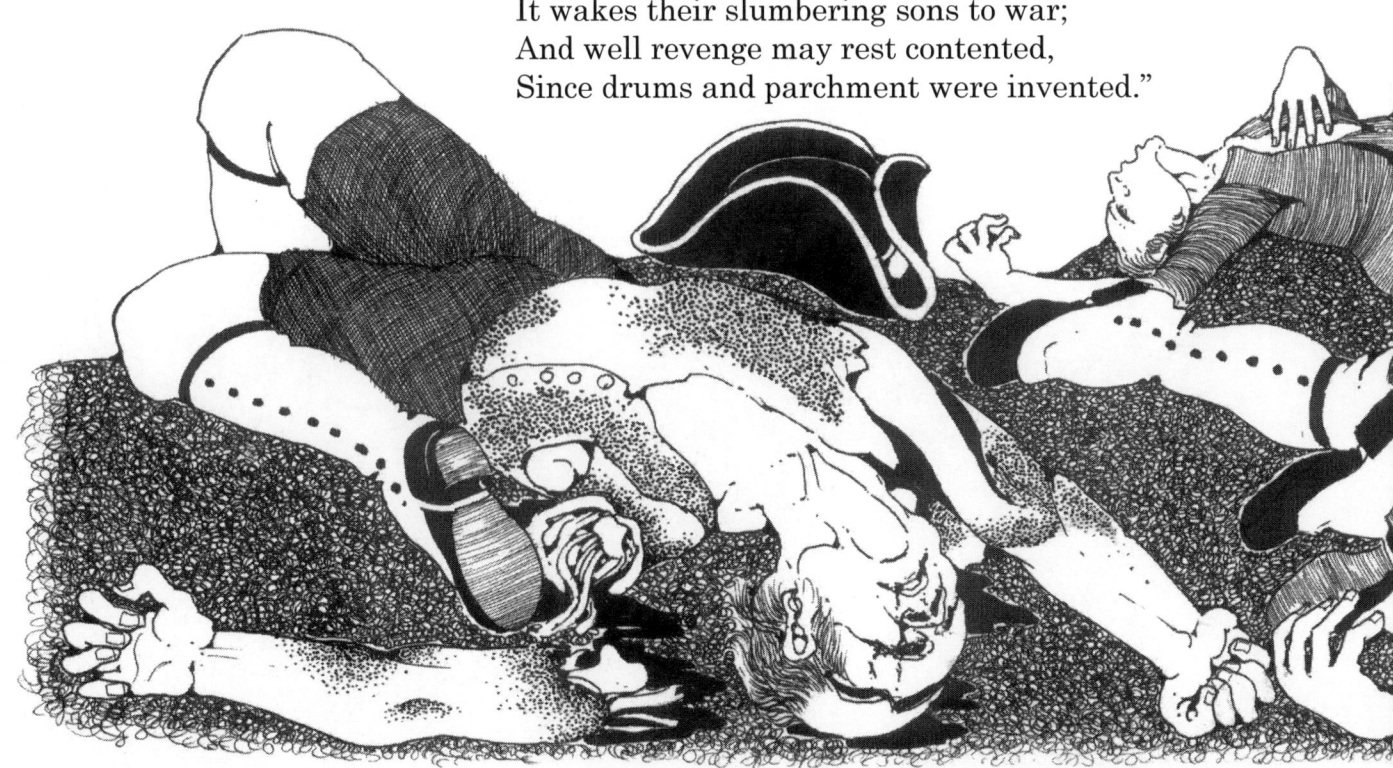

FABLE 6

The Miser and Plutus

The wind was high, the window shakes,
With sudden start the Miser wakes;
Along the silent room he stalks,
Looks back, and trembles as he walks.
Each lock and every bolt he tries,
In every creek and corner pries;
Then opes the chest with treasure stored,
And stands in rapture o'er his hoard:
But now with sudden qualms possest,
He wrings his hands he beats his breast;
By conscience stung he wildly stares,
And thus his guilty soul declares:
   "Had the deep earth her stores confined.
This heart had known sweet peace of mind.
But virtue's sold. Good gods! what price
Can recompense the pangs of vice!
O bane of good! seducing cheat!
Can man, weak man, thy power defeat?
Gold banish'd honour from the mind,
And only left the name behind;
Gold sow'd the world with every ill;
Gold taught the murderer's sword to kill:

'Twas gold instructed coward hearts
In treachery's more pernicious arts.
Who can recount the mischiefs o'er?
Virtue resides on earth no more!"
He spoke, and sigh'd. In angry mood,
Plutus, his god, before him stood.
The Miser, trembling, lock'd his chest;
The vision frown'd, and thus address'd:
 "Whence is this vile ungrateful rant,
Each sordid meal's daily cant?
Did I, base wretch! corrupt mankind?
The fault's in thy rapacious mind.
Because my blessings are abused,
Must I be censured, cursed, accused?
Ev'n Virtue's self by knaves is made
A cloak to carry on the trade;
And power (when lodged in their possession)
Grows tyranny, and rank oppression.
Thus, when the villain crams his chest,
Gold is the canker of the breast,
'Tis avarice, insolence, and pride,
And every shocking vice beside;
But when to virtuous hands 'tis given,
It blesses, like the dews of Heaven:
Like Heaven, it hears the orphan's cries,
And wipes the tears from widows' eyes.
Their crimes on gold shall misers lay,
Who pawn'd their sordid souls for pay?
Let bravos, then, when blood is spilt,
Upbraid the passive sword with guilt."

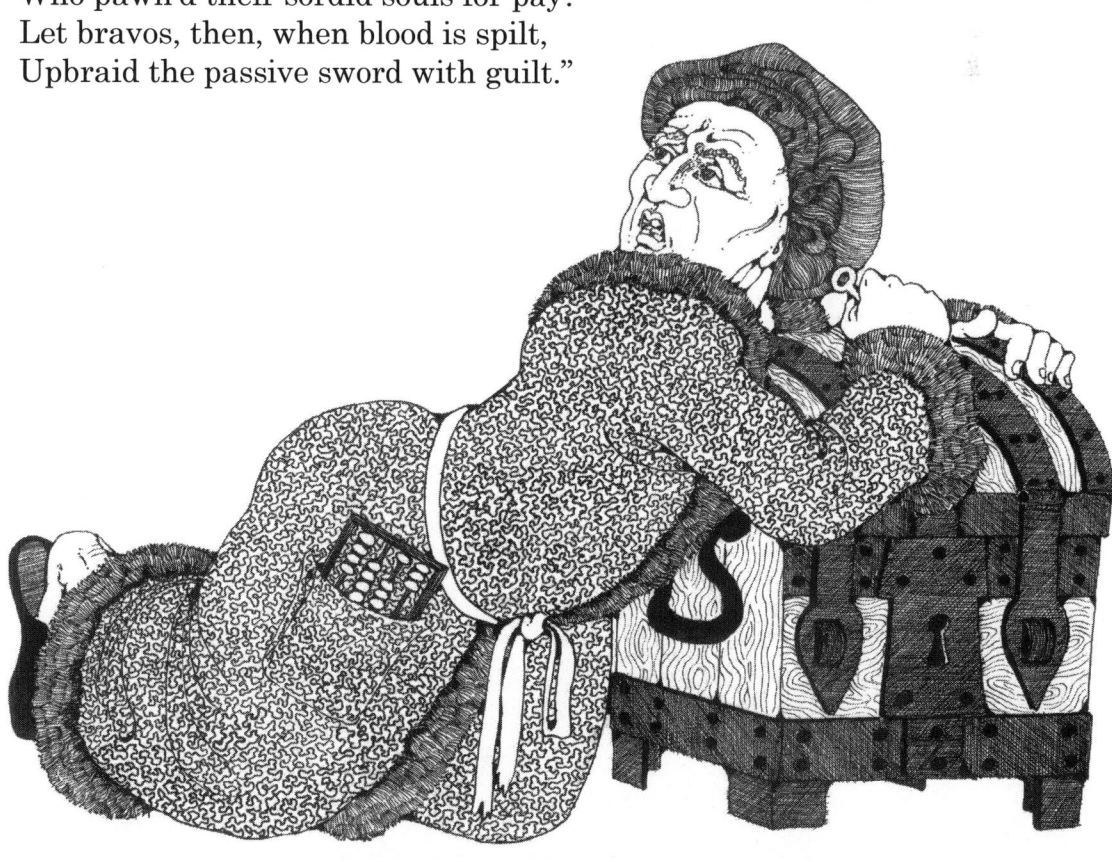

FABLE 7

The Lion, the Fox, and the Geese

A Lion, tired with state affairs,
Quite sick of pomp, and worn with cares,
Resolv'd (remote from noise and strife)
In peace to pass his latter life.
　　It was proclaimed; the day was set;
Behold the general council met.
The Fox was Viceroy named. The crowd
To the new Regent humbly bow'd.
Wolves, bears, and mighty tigers bend,

And strive who most shall condescend.
He straight assumes a solemn grace,
Collects his wisdom in his face:
The crowd admire his wit, his sense:
Each word hath weight and consequence.
The flatterer all his art displays:
He who hath power is sure of praise!
A Fox stept forth before the rest,
And thus the servile throng addrest:
  "How vast his talents, born to rule,
And train'd in Virtue's honest school!
What clemency his temper sways!
How uncorrupt are all his ways!
Beneath his conduct and command
Rapine shall cease to waste the land.
His brain hath stratagem and art;
Prudence and mercy rule his heart.
What blessings must attend the nation
Under this good administration!"
He said. A Goose, who distant stood,
Harangued apart the cackling brood.
  "Whene'er I hear a knave commend,
He bids me shun his worthy friend.
What praise, what mighty commendation!
But 'twas a Fox who spoke the oration.
Foxes this government may prize
As gentle, plentiful, and wise;
If they enjoy the sweets, 'tis plain
We Geese must feel a tyrant reign.
What havoc now shall thin our race,
When every petty clerk in place,
To prove his taste, and seem polite,
Will feed on Geese both noon and night."

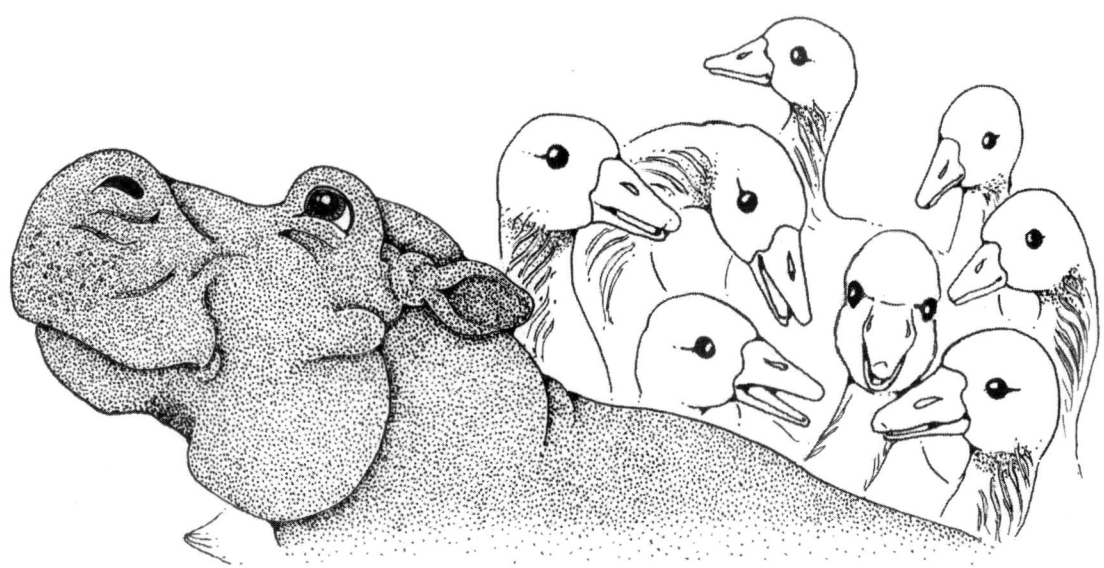

FABLE 8

The Lady and the Wasp

What whispers must the Beauty bear!
What hourly nonsense haunts her ear!
Where'er her eyes dispense their charms,
Impertinence around her swarms.
Did not the tender nonsense strike,
Contempt and scorn might look dislike;
Forbidding airs might thin the place,
The slightest flap a fly can chase:
But who can drive the num'rous breed?
Chase one, another will succeed;
Who knows a fool, must know his brother;
One fop will recommend another:
And with this plague she's rightly curst,
Because she listen'd to the first.
   As Doris, at her toilette's duty,
Sat meditating on her beauty,
She now was pensive, now was gay,
And loll'd the sultry hours away.
   As thus in indolence she lies,
A giddy Wasp around her flies:
He now advances, now retires,
Now to her neck and cheek aspires.
Her fan in vain defends her charms;
Swift he returns, again alarms;
For by repulse he bolder grew,
Perch'd on her lip, and sipt the dew.
   She frowns, she frets. "Good gods!" she cries,
"Protect me from these teasing flies!
Of all the plagues that heaven hath sent,
A Wasp is most impertinent."
   The hovering insect thus complain'd,
"Am I then slighted, scorn'd, disdain'd?
Can such offence your anger wake?

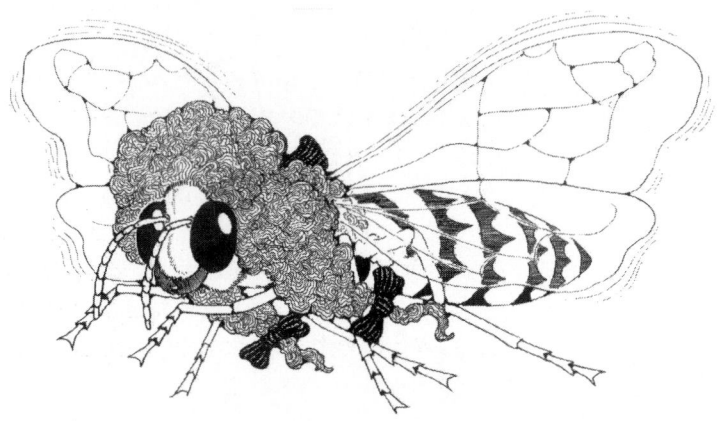

Twas beauty caused the bold mistake.
The fairest peach that ever grew."
Those cherry lips that breathe perfume,
That cheek so ripe with youthful bloom,
Made me with strong desire pursue
  "Strike him not, Jenny!" Doris cries,
"Nor murder Wasps like vulgar flies;
For though he's free (to do him right),
The creature's civil and polite.
  In ecstasies, away he posts;
Where'er he came, the favour boasts;
Brags, how her sweetest tea he sips,
And shows the sugar on his lips.
  The hint alarm'd the forward crew
Sure of success, away they flew.
They share the dainties of the day,
Round her with airy music play:
And now they flutter, now they rest,
Now soar again, and skim her breast.
Nor were they banish'd till she found
That Wasps have stings, and felt the wound.

FABLE 9

The Bull and the Mastiff

Seek you to train your favourite boy?
Each caution, every care employ;
And ere you venture to confide,
Let his preceptor's heart be tried:
Weigh well his manners, life, and scope;
On these depends thy future hope.
   As on a time, in peaceful reign,
A Bull enjoy'd the flowery plain,
A Mastiff pass'd; inflamed with ire,
His eyeballs shot indignant fire;
He foam'd, he raged with thirst of blood.

Spurning the ground, the monarch stood,
And roar'd aloud: "Suspend the fight;
In a whole skin go sleep to-night;
Or tell me, ere the battle rage,
What wrongs provoke thee to engage?
Is it ambition fires thy breast,
Or avarice, that ne'er can rest?
From these alone unjustly springs
The world-destroying wrath of kings."
  The surly Mastiff thus returns:
Within my bosom, glory burns.
Like heroes of eternal name,
Whom poets sing, I fight for fame.
The butcher's spirit-stirring mind
To daily war my youth inclined;
He train'd me to heroic deed,
Taught me to conquer or to bleed."
  "Curs'd Dog," the Bull replied, "no more
I wonder at thy thirst of gore;
For thou (beneath a butcher train'd,
Whose hands with cruelty are stain'd,
His daily murders in thy view)
Must, like thy tutor, blood pursue.
Take, then, thy fate!" With goring wound
At once he lifts him from the ground:
Aloft the sprawling hero flies,
Mangled he falls, he howls, and dies.

FABLE 10

The Elephant and the Bookseller

The man who with undaunted toils
Sails unknown seas to unknown soils,
With various wonders feasts his sight:
What stranger wonders does he write?
We read, and in description view
Creatures which Adam never knew;
For when we risk no contradiction,
It prompts the tongue to deal in fiction.
Those things that startle me or you,
I grant are strange, yet may be true.
Who doubts that Elephants are found
For science and for sense renown'd?
Borri records their strength of parts,
Extent of thought, and skill in arts;
How they perform the law's decrees,
And save the state, the hangman's fees;
And how by travel understand
The language of another land.

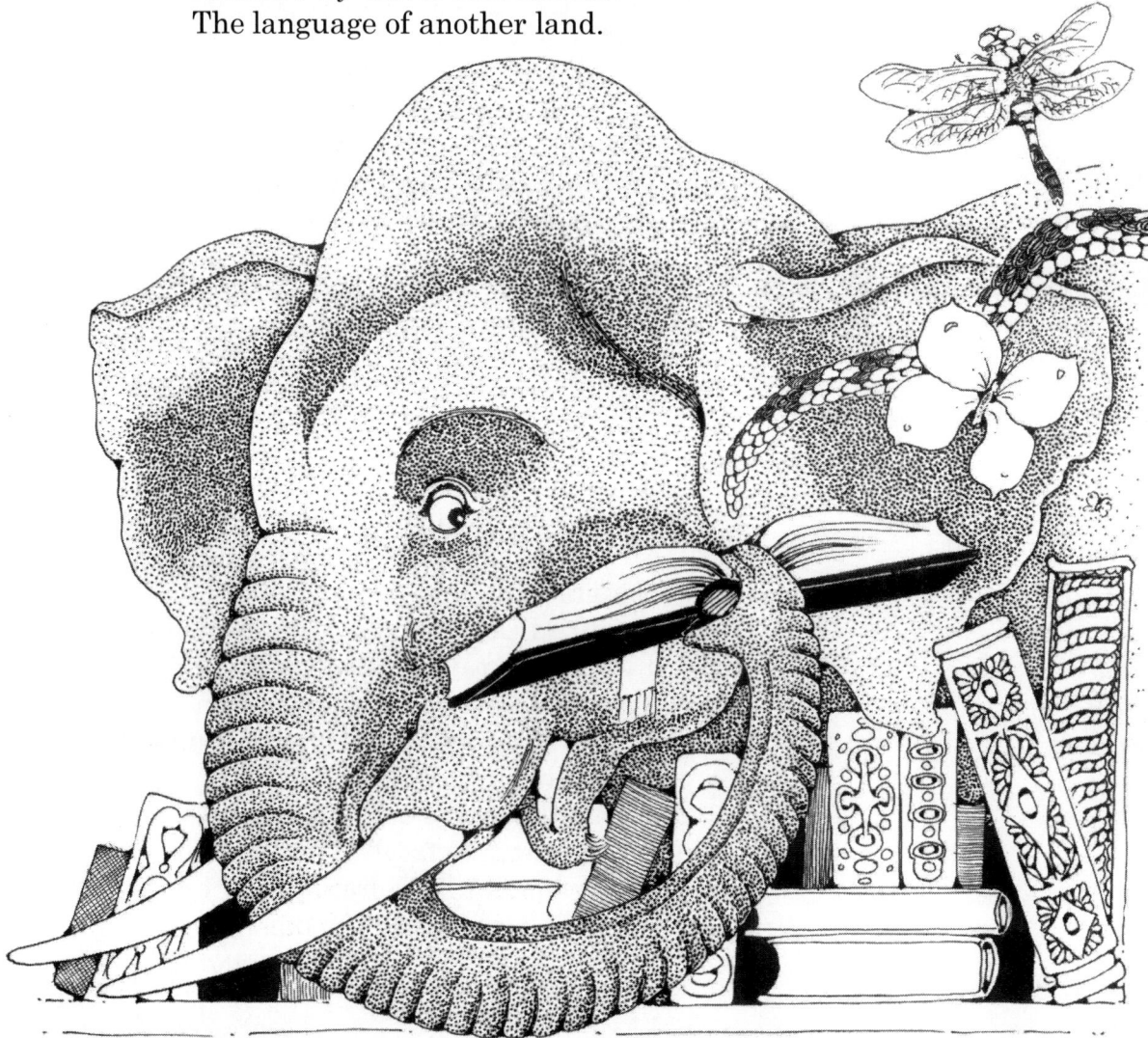

Let those who question this report,
To Pliny's ancient page resort.
How learn'd was that sagacious breed!
Who now (like them), the Greek can read?
  As one of these, in days of yore,
Rummaged a shop of learning o'er;
Not, like our modern dealers, minding
Only the margin's breadth and binding;
A book his curious eye detains,
Where, with exactest care and pains,
Were every beast and bird portray'd,
That e'er the search of man survey'd;
Their natures and their powers were writ
With all the pride of human wit.
The page, he, with attention spread,
And thus remark'd on what he read:
  "Man with strong reason is endow'd,
A beast, scarce instinct is allow'd:
But let this author's worth be tried,
Tis plain that neither was his guide.
Can he discern the different natures,
And weigh the power of other creatures,
Who by the partial work hath shown
He knows so little of his own?
How falsely is the spaniel drawn!
Did man from him, first learn to fawn?
A dog, proficient in the trade,
He, the chief flatterer Nature made!
Go, Man! the ways of courts discern,
You'll find a spaniel still might learn.
How can the fox's theft and plunder
Provoke his censure or his wonder?
From courtiers' tricks and lawyers' arts,
The fox might well improve his parts.
The lion, wolf, and tiger's brood,
He curses, for their thirst of blood:
But is not man to man a prey?

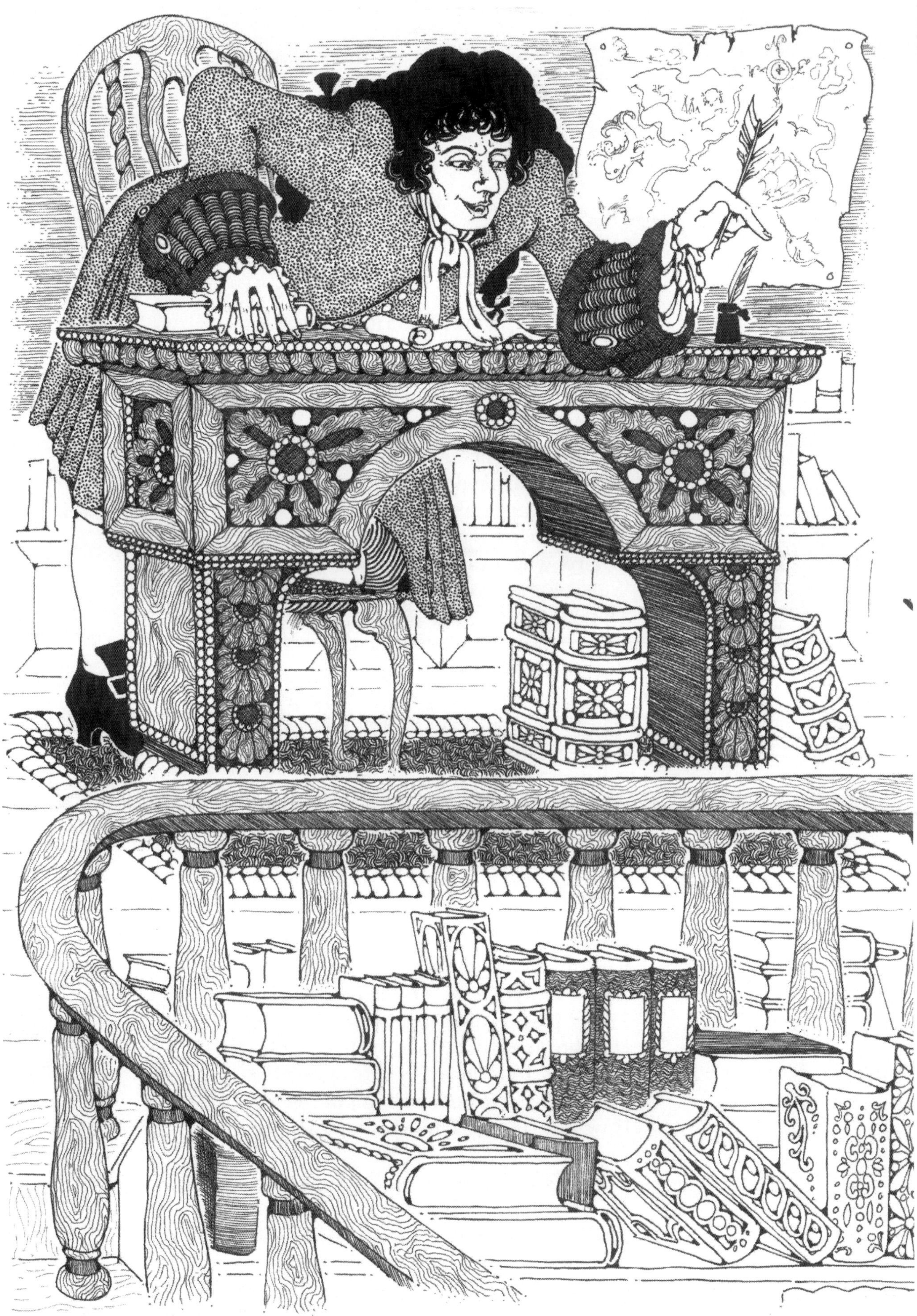

Beasts kill for hunger, men for pay."
The Bookseller, who heard him speak,
And saw him turn a page of Greek,
Thought, "What a genius have I found!"
Then thus address'd with bow profound:
  "Learn'd Sir, if you'd employ your pen
Against the senseless sons of men,
Or write the history of Siam,
No man is better pay than I am;
Or, since you're learn'd in Greek, let's see
Something against the Trinity."
  When wrinkling with a sneer, his trunk,
"Friend," quoth the Elephant, "you're drunk;
E'en keep your money, and be wise:
Leave man on man, to criticise;
For that you ne'er can want a pen,
Among the senseless sons of men.
They unprovok'd, will court the fray:
Envy's a sharper spur than pay.
No author ever spared a brother;
Wits are game-cocks, to one another.

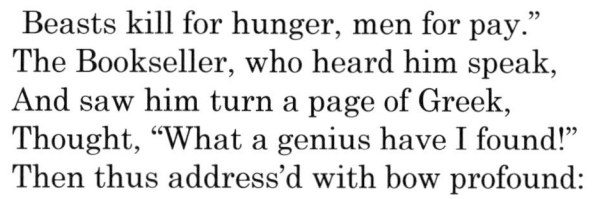

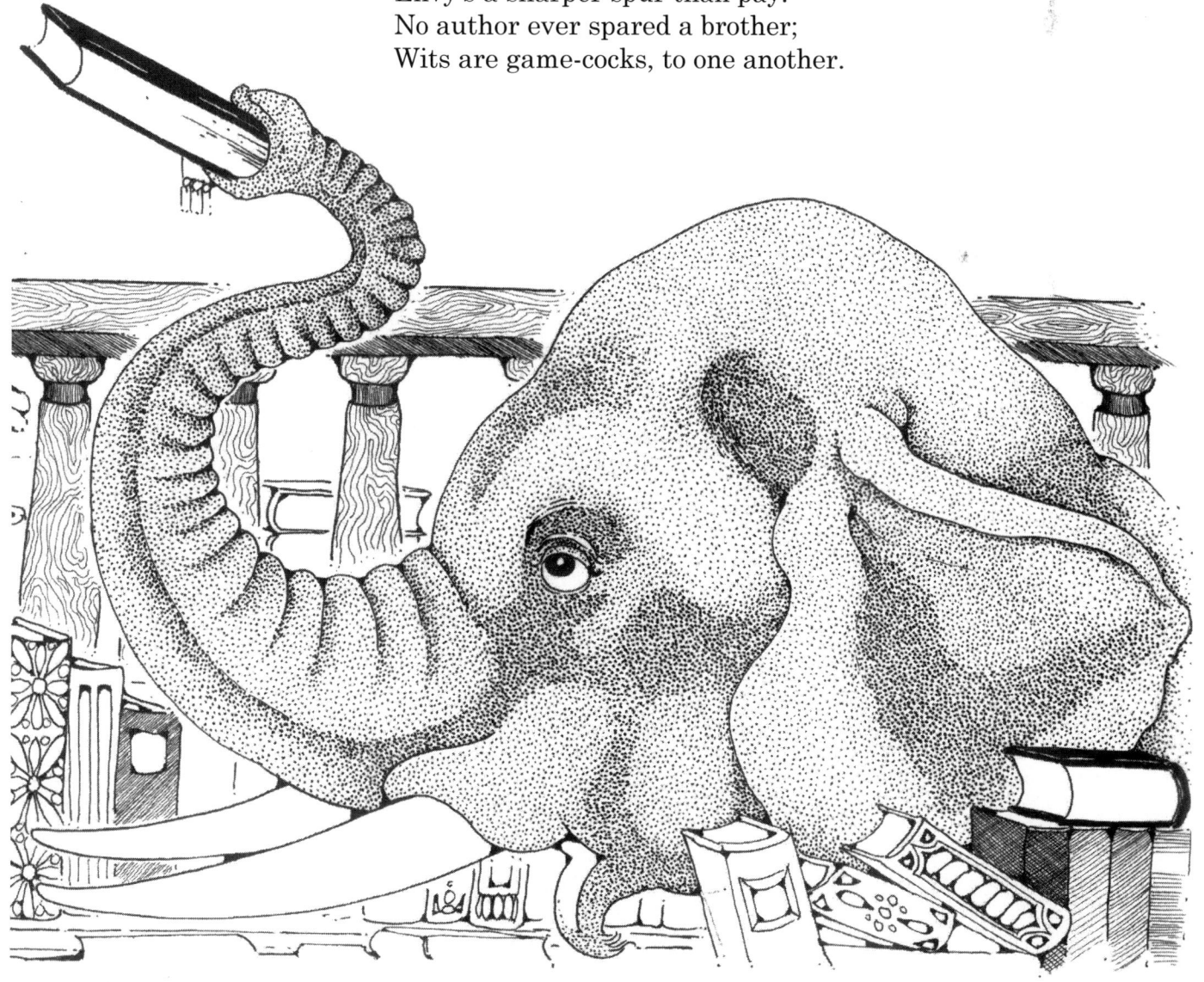

FABLE 11

The Peacock, the Turkey, and the Goose

In beauty, faults conspicuous grow;
The smallest speck is seen on snow.
   As near a barn, by hunger led,
A Peacock with the poultry fed,
All view'd him with an envious eye,
And mock'd his gaudy pageantry.
He, conscious of superior merit,
Contemns their base reviling spirit;
His state and dignity assumes,
And to the sun displays his plumes,
Which, like the heaven's o'er-arching skies,
Are spangled with a thousand eyes,
The circling rays, and varied light,
At once confound their dazzled sight;
On every tongue detraction burns,
And malice prompts their spleen by turns.
   "Mark with what insolence and pride
The creature takes his haughty stride,"
The Turkey cries. "Can spleen contain?
Sure never bird was half so vain!
But were intrinsic merit seen,
We Turkeys have the whiter skin."

  From tongue to tongue they caught abuse,
And next was heard the hissing Goose:
"What hideous legs! what filthy claws!
I scorn to censure little flaws;
Then what a horrid squalling throat!
Ev'n owls are frighted at the note."
  "True. Those are faults," the Peacock cries,
"My scream, my shanks, you may despise;
But such blind critics rail in vain;
What, overlook my radiant train!
Know, did my legs (your scorn and sport),
The Turkey, or the Goose, support,
And did ye scream with harsher sound,
Those faults in you, had ne'er been found:
To all apparent beauties blind,
Each blemish strikes an envious mind."
Thus in assemblies have I seen
A nymph, of brightest charms and mien,
Wake envy in each ugly face,
And buzzing scandal fills the place.

FABLE 12

Cupid, Hymen and Plutus

As Cupid in Cythera's grove
Employ'd the lesser powers of Love;
Some shape the bow, or fit the string,
Some give the taper shaft its wing,
Or turn the polish'd quiver's mould,
Or head the darts with temper'd gold.
   Amidst their toil and various care
Thus Hymen, with assuming air,
Address'd the god: "Thou purblind chit,
Of awkward and ill-judging wit,
If matches are no better made,
At once I must forswear my trade
You send me such ill-coupled folks,
That 'tis a shame to sell them yokes.
They squabble for a pin, a feather,
And wonder how they came together.
The husband's sullen, dogged, shy,
The wife grows flippant in reply:
He loves command and due restriction,
And she as well likes contradiction:

She never slavishly submits,
She'll have her will, or have her fits
He this way tugs, she t'other draws;
The man grows jealous, and with cause;
Nothing can save him but divorce,
And here the wife complies of course."

"When," says the boy, "had I to do
With either your affairs, or you?
I never idly spend my darts:
You trade in mercenary hearts.
For settlements the lawyer's fee'd;
Is my hand witness to the deed?
If they like cat and dog agree.
Go rail at Plutus, not at me."

Plutus appear'd, and said, "'Tis true,
In marriage, gold is all their view;
They seek not beauty, wit, or sense,
And love is seldom the pretence.
All offer incense at my shrine,
And I alone the bargain sign.
How can Belinda blame her fate?
She only ask'd a great estate.
Doris was rich enough, 'tis true,
Her lord must give her title too;
And every man, or rich or poor,
A fortune asks, and asks no more."

Avarice, whatever shape it bears,
Must still be coupled with its cares.

FABLE 13

The Tame Stag

As a young Stag the thicket past,
The branches held his antlers fast;
A clown, who saw the captive hung,
Across the horns his halter flung.
  Now safely hamper'd in the cord,
He bore the present to his lord.
His lord was pleased, as was the clown,
When he was tipp'd with half-a-crown.
The Stag was brought before his wife;
The tender lady begg'd his life;
"How sleek's the skin! how speck'd like ermine!
Sure never creature was so charming!"

At first within the yard confined,
He flies and hides from all mankind;
Now bolder grown, with fix'd amaze,
And distant awe, presumes to gaze;
Munches the linen on the lines,
And on a hood or apron dines,
He steals my little master's bread,
Follows the servants to be fed,
Nearer and nearer now he stands,
To feel the praise of patting hands;
Examines every fist for meat,
And, though repulsed, disdains retreat;
Attacks again with levell'd horns,
And man, that was his terror, scorns.
Such is the country maiden's fright,
When first a red-coat is in sight;
Behind the door she hides her face,
Next time, at distance, eyes the lace.
She now can all his terrors stand,
Nor from his squeeze withdraws her hand.
She plays familiar in his arms,
And every soldier hath his charms:
From tent to tent she spreads her flame;
For custom conquers fear and shame.

FABLE 14

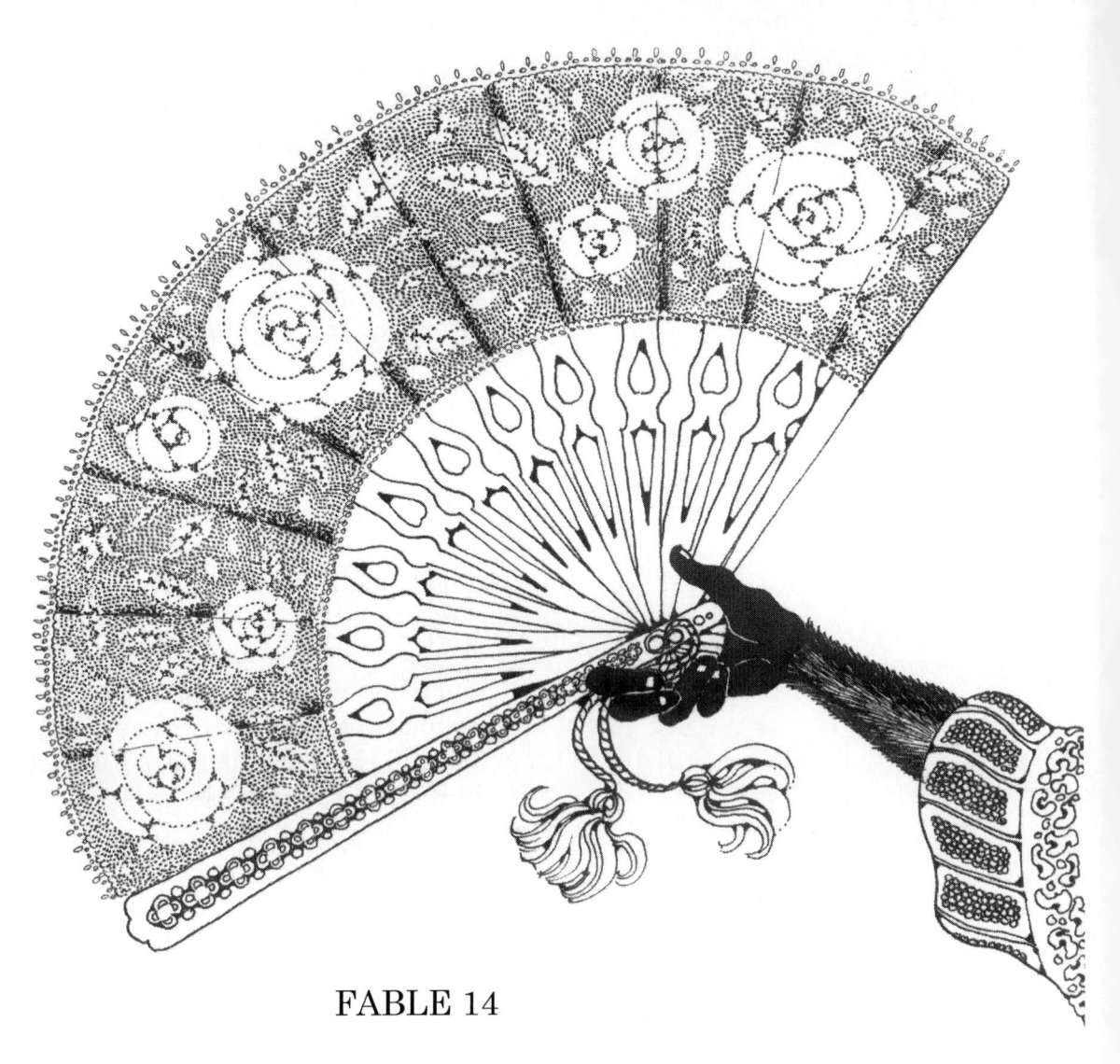

The Monkey Who Had Seen the World

A Monkey, to reform the times,
Resolved to visit foreign climes;
For men in distant regions roam
To bring politer manners home.
So forth he fares, all toil defies:
Misfortune serves to make us wise.
  At length the treacherous snare was laid;
Poor Pug was caught; to town convey'd;
There sold. (How envied was his doom,
Made captive in a lady's room!)
Proud, as a lover, of his chains,
He, day by day, her favour gains.
Whene'er the duty of the day
The toilet calls, with mimic play
He twirls her knots, he cracks her fan,
Like any other gentleman.
In visits, too, his parts and wit,
When jests grew dull, were sure to hit.

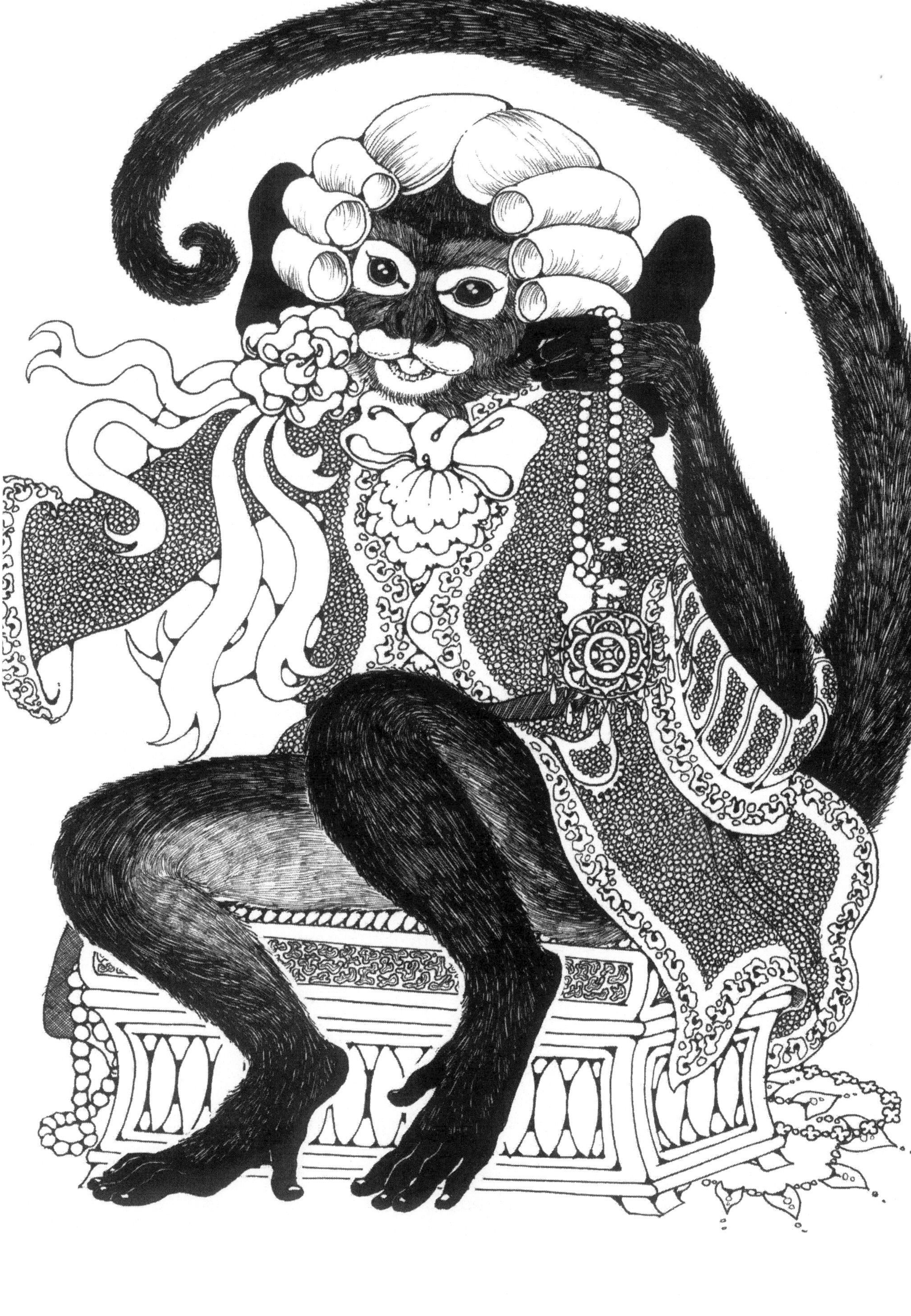

Proud with applause, he thought his mind
In every courtly art refined;
Like Orpheus, burnt with public zeal,
To civilise the monkey weal;
So watch'd occasion, broke his chain,
And sought his native woods again.
The hairy sylvans round him press,
Astonish'd at his strut and dress:
Some praise his sleeve, and others gloat
Upon his rich embroider'd coat.
His dapper periwig commending,
With the black tail behind depending;
His powder'd back, above, below,
Like hoary frosts, or fleecy snow;
But all, with envy and desire,
His fluttering shoulder-knot admire.
  "Hear and improve," he pertly cries,
"I come to make a nation wise.
Weigh your own worth; support your place,
The next in rank to human race.
In cities long I pass'd my days,
Conversed with men, and learn'd their ways.
Their dress, their courtly manners see;
Reform your state, and copy me.

Seek ye to thrive? In flattery deal;
Your scorn, your hate, with that conceal.
Seem only to regard your friends,
But use them for your private ends.
Stint not to truth the flow of wit,
Be prompt to lie, whene'er 'tis fit.
Bend all your force to spatter merit;
Scandal is conversation's spirit.
Boldly to everything pretend,
And men your talents shall commend.
I knew the great. Observe me right;
So shall you grow, like man, polite."
   He spoke and bow'd. With muttering jaws,
The wondering circle grinn'd applause.
   Now, warm'd with malice, envy, spite,
Their most obliging friends they bite;
And fond to copy human ways,
Practise new mischiefs all their days.
Thus the dull lad, too tall for school,
With travel finishes the fool;
Studious of every coxcomb's airs,
He drinks, games, dresses, whores, and swears;
O'erlooks with scorn all virtuous arts,
For vice is fitted to his parts.

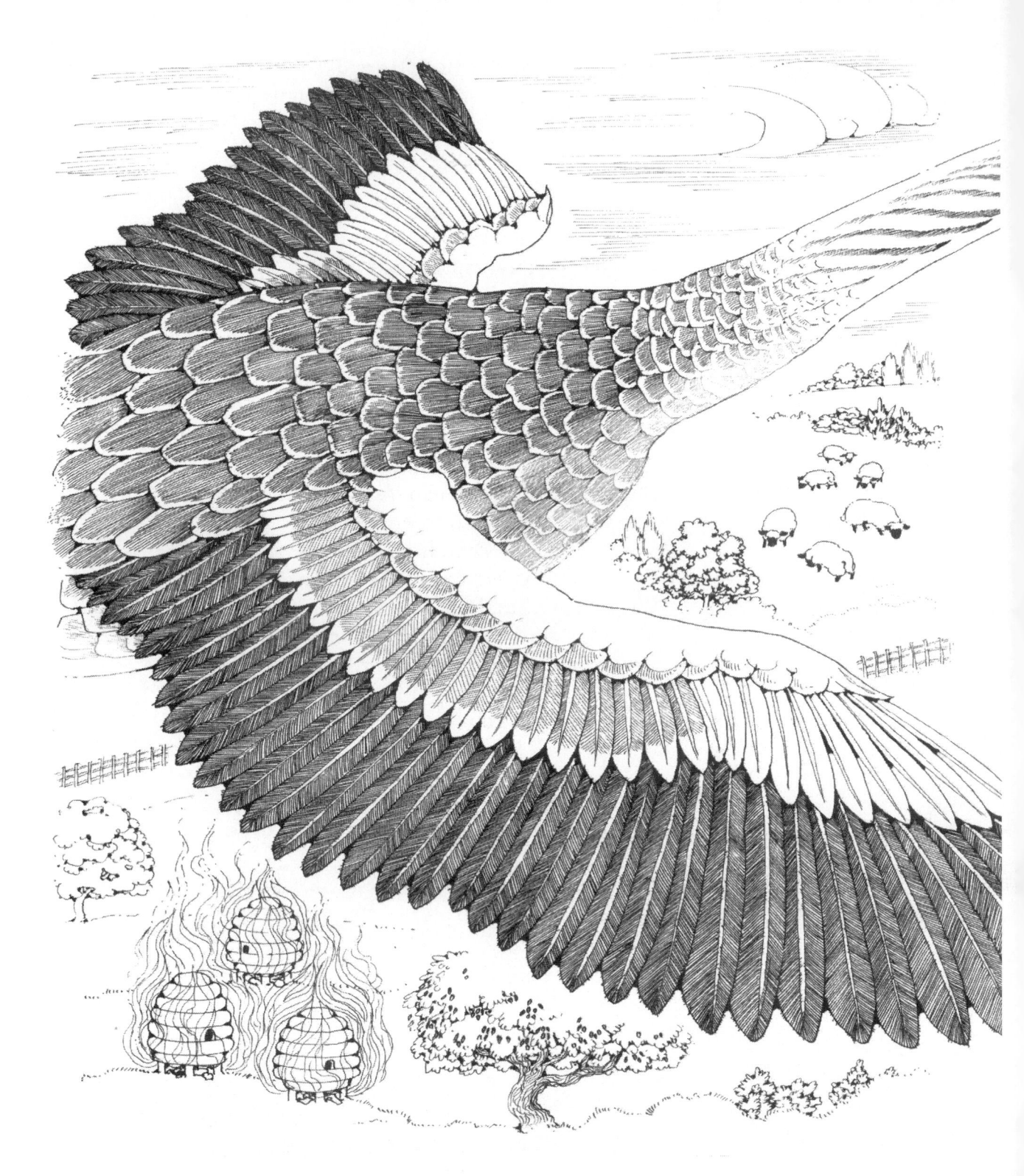

FABLE 15

The Philosopher and the Pheasants

> The Sage, awaked at early day,
> Through the deep forest took his way;
> Drawn by the music of the groves,
> Along the winding gloom he roves;

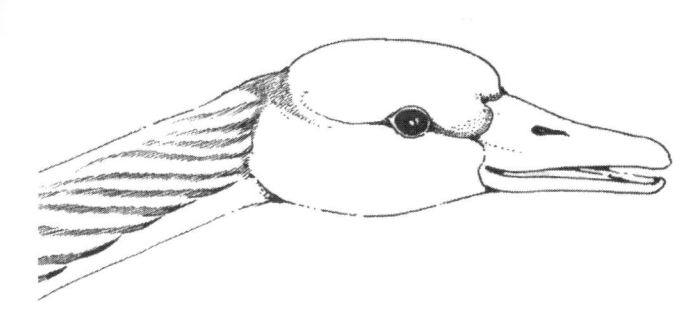

From tree to tree the warbling throats
Prolong the sweet alternate notes.
But where he past, he terror threw,
The song broke short, the warblers flew;
The thrushes chatter'd with affright,
And nightingales abhorr'd his sight;
All animals before him ran,
To shun the hateful sight of man.
　"Whence is this dread of every creature?
Fly they our figure or our nature?"
　As thus he walk'd in musing thought,
His ear imperfect accents caught.
With cautious step he nearer drew,
By the thick shade conceal'd from view.
High on the branch a Pheasant stood,
Around her all her listening brood;
Proud of the blessings of her nest,
She thus a mother's care express'd:
　"No dangers here shall circumvent;
Within the woods enjoy content.
Sooner the hawk or vulture trust
Than man, of animals the worst:
In him ingratitude you find,
A vice peculiar to the kind.
The sheep, whose annual fleece is dyed,
To guard his health, and serve his pride;
Forced from his fold and native plain,
Is, in the cruel shambles, slain.
The swarms who, with industrious skill,
His hives with wax and honey fill,
In vain whole summer days employ'd;
Their stores are sold, the race destroy'd.
What tribute from the goose is paid!
Does not her wing all science aid?
(Does it not lovers' hearts explain)
And drudge to raise the merchant's gain?
What now rewards this general use?
He takes the quills, and eats the goose.
Man then avoid, detest his ways,
So safety shall prolong your days.
When services are thus acquitted,
Be sure we Pheasants must be spitted."

FABLE 16

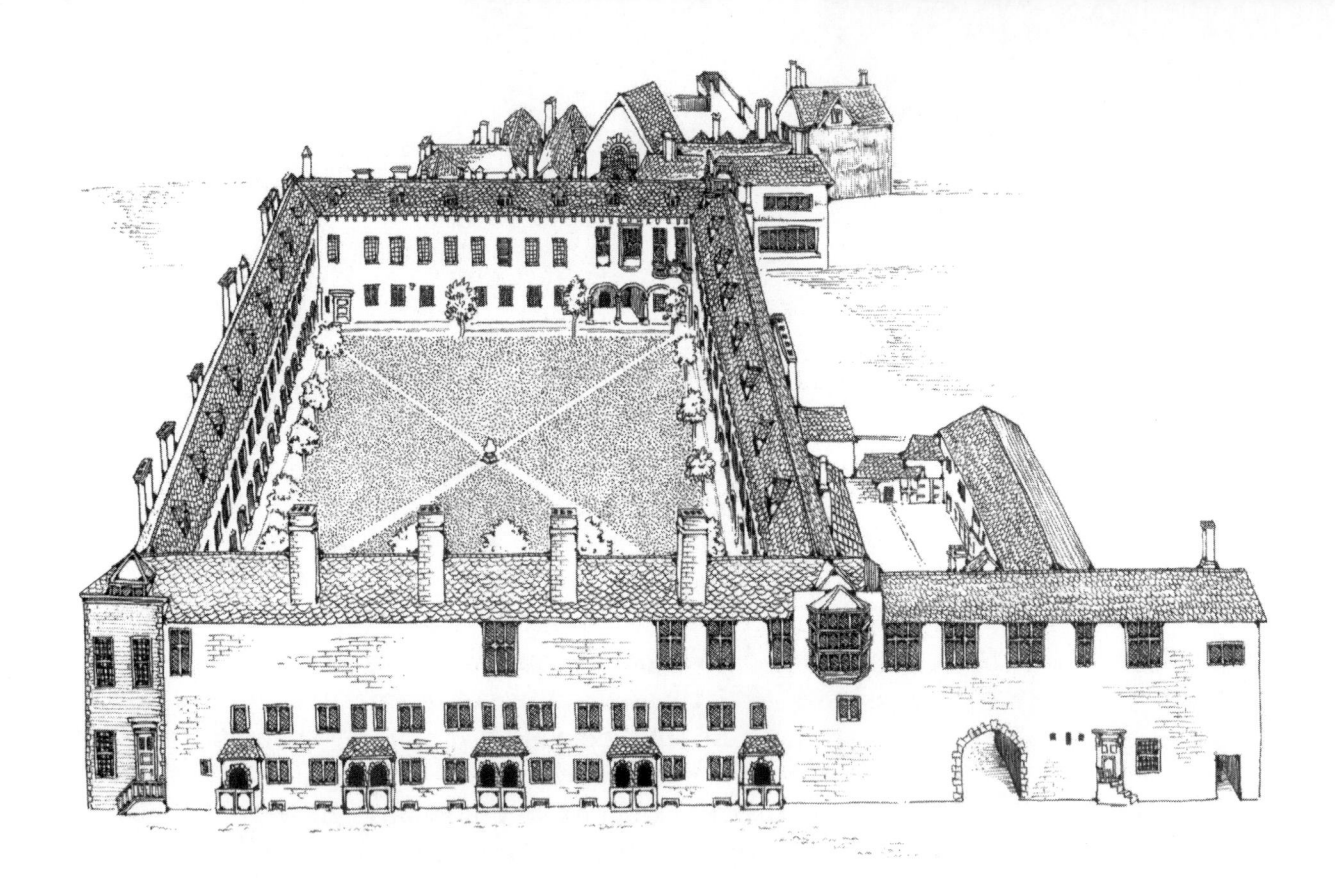

The Pin and the Needle

A Pin who long had served a beauty,
Proficient in the toilet's duty,
Had form'd her sleeve, confined her hair;
Or given her knot a smarter air;
Now nearest to her heart was placed
Now in her manteau's tail disgraced;
But could she partial fortune blame,
Who saw her lovers, served the same?
   At length from all her honours cast,
Through various turns of life she past:
Now glitter'd on a tailor's arm,
Now kept a beggar's infant warm;
Now, ranged within a miser's coat,
Contributes to his yearly groat;
Now, raised again from low approach,
She visits in the doctor's coach:
Here, there, by various fortune tost,
At last in Gresham Hall was lost.
   Charm'd with the wonders of the show,
On every side, above, below,
She now of this or that, inquires,
What least was understood, admires.

'Tis plain each thing so struck her mind,
Her head's of virtuoso kind.
   "And pray what's this, and this, dear Sir?"
"A needle," says the interpreter.
She knew the name; and thus the fool
Address'd her, as a tailor's tool:
   "A needle with that filthy stone,
Quite idle, all with rust o'ergrown:
You better might employ your parts,
And aid the semstress in her arts.
But tell me how the friendship grew
Between that paltry flint and you?"
   "Friend," says the Needle, "cease to blame;
I follow real worth and fame.
Know'st thou the loadstone's power and art,
That virtue, virtues can impart?
Of all his talents I partake,
Who then can such a friend forsake?
'Tis I direct the pilot's hand
To shun the rocks and treacherous sand:
By me the distant world is known,
And either India is our own.
Had I with milliners been bred,
What had I been? the guide of thread,
And drudged as vulgar Needles do,
Of no more consequence than you."

FABLE 17

The Shepherd's Dog and the Wolf

A Wolf, with hunger, fierce and bold,
Ravaged the plains, and thinn'd the fold;
Deep in the wood, secure he lay,
The thefts of night regaled the day.
In vain the shepherd's wakeful care
Had spread the toils, and watch'd the snare;
In vain the dog pursued his pace,
The fleeter robber mock'd the chase.
  As Lightfoot ranged the forest round,
By chance his foe's retreat he found.
  "Let us awhile the war suspend,
And reason as from friend to friend."
  "A truce!" replies the Wolf. 'Tis done.
The Dog the parley thus begun:
  "How can that strong intrepid mind
Attack a weak defenceless kind?
Those jaws should prey on nobler food,
And drink the boar's and lion's blood.
Great souls with generous pity melt,
Which coward tyrants never felt.
How harmless is our fleecy care!
Be brave, and let thy mercy spare."
  "Friend," says the wolf, "the matter weigh;
Nature design'd us beasts of prey;
As such, when hunger finds a treat,
'Tis necessary Wolves should eat.
If, mindful of the bleating weal,
Thy bosom burn with real zeal,
Hence, and thy tyrant lord beseech;
To him repeat the moving speech:
A Wolf eats Sheep but now and then,
Ten thousands are devour'd by men.
An open foe may prove a curse
But a pretended friend is worse."

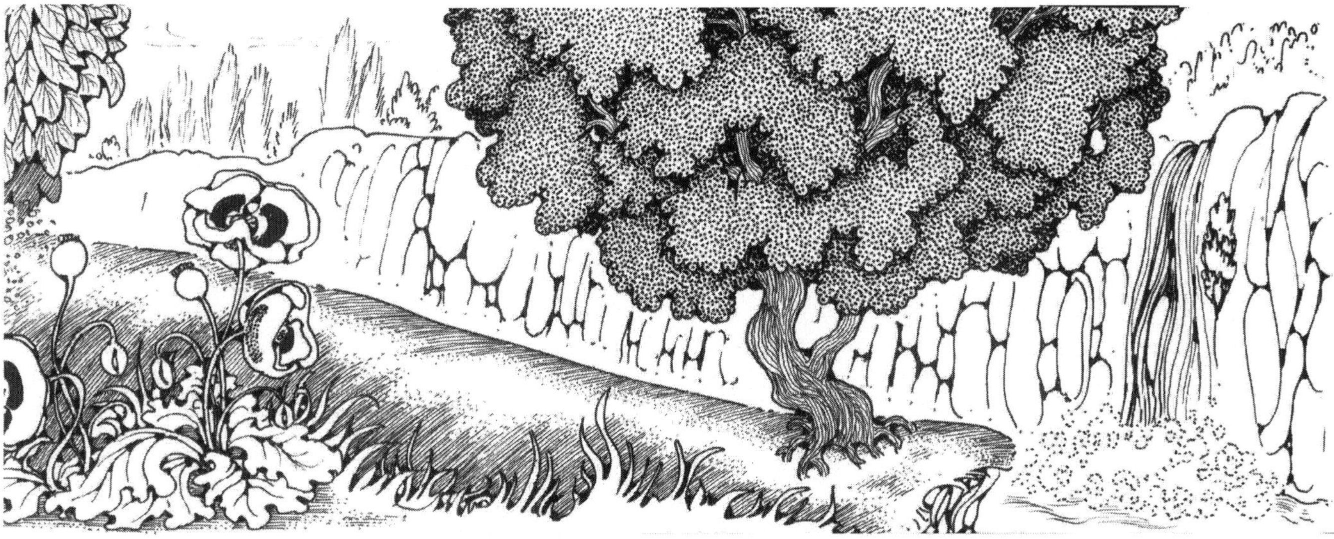

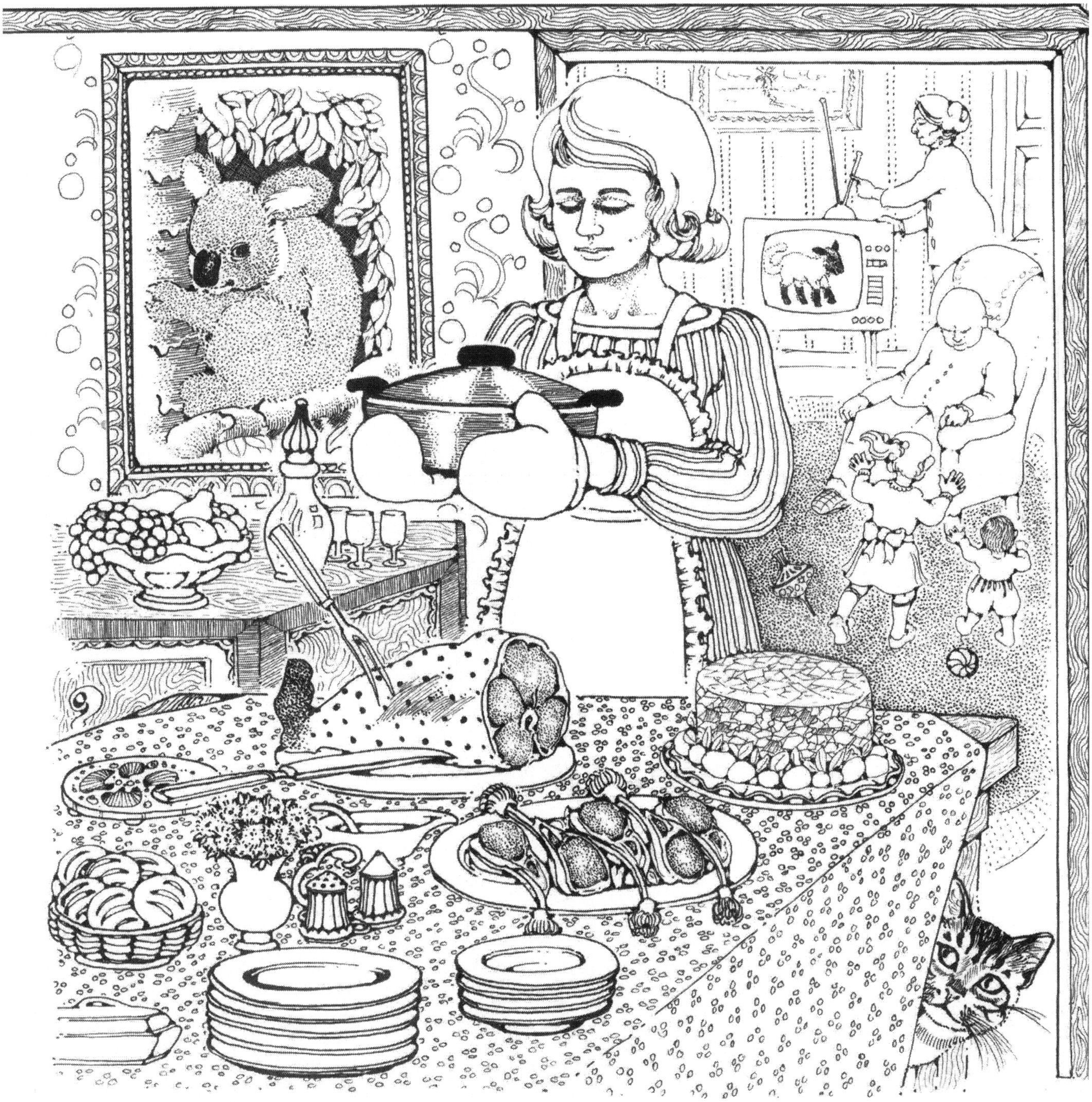

FABLE 18

The Painter Who Pleased Nobody and Everybody

Lest men suspect your tale untrue,
Keep probability in view.
The traveller leaping o'er those bounds,
The credit of his book confounds.
Who with his tongue hath armies routed,
Makes ev'n his real courage doubted.
But flattery never seems absurd;
The flatter'd always take your word:
Impossibilities seem just,
They take the strongest praise on trust.
Hyperboles, though ne'er so great,
Will still come short of self-conceit.
   So very like, a painter drew,
That every eye, the picture knew.
He hit complexion, feature, air,
So just, the life itself was there.

No flattery with his colours laid,
To bloom restored the faded maid;
He gave each muscle all its strength;
The mouth, the chin, the nose's length;
His honest pencil touch'd with truth.
And mark'd the date of age and youth.
   He lost his friends, his practice fail'd;
Truth should not always be reveal'd.
In dusty piles his pictures lay,
For no one sent the second pay.
   Two bustos, fraught with every grace,
A Venus' and Apollo's face,
He placed in view; resolved to please,
Whoever sat, he drew from these,
From these corrected every feature,
And spirited each awkward creature.

All things were set, the hour was come,
His pallet ready o'er his thumb;
My Lord appear'd, and seated right,
In proper attitude and light,
The Painter look'd, he sketch'd the piece,
Then dipt his pencil, talk'd of Greece,
Of Titian's tints, of Guido's air;
   "Those eyes, my Lord, the spirit there
Might well a Raphael's hand require,
To give them all the native fire.
The features, fraught with sense and wit,
You'll grant are very hard to hit;
But yet with patience you shall view
As much as paint and art can do."
   "Observe the work!" My Lord replied,
"Till now I thought my mouth was wide;
Besides, my nose is somewhat long:
Dear Sir, for me, 'tis far too young."
   "Oh! pardon me," (the artist cried)
"In this, we Painters must decide.

The piece, e'en common eyes must strike;
I warrant it extremely like."
   My Lord examined it anew;
No looking-glass seem'd half so true.
   A lady came, with borrow'd grace
He, from his Venus, form'd her face.
Her lover praised the painter's art;
So like the picture in his heart!
To every age, some charm he lent;
E'en beauties were almost content.
Through all the town his art they praised;
His custom grew, his price was raised.
Had he the real likeness shown,
Would any man the picture own?
But when thus happily he wrought,
Each found the likeness in his thought.

FABLE 19

The Lion and the Cub

How fond are men of rule and place,
Who court it from the mean and base!
These cannot bear an equal nigh,
But from superior merit fly.
They love the cellar's vulgar joke,
And lose their hours in ale and smoke.
There o'er some petty club preside;
So poor, so paltry, is their pride!
Nay, e'en with fools, whole nights will sit,
In hopes to be supreme in wit.
If these can read, to these I write,
To set their worth in truest light.
  A Lion-cub, of sordid mind,
Avoided all the lion kind;
Fond of applause, he sought the feasts
Of vulgar and ignoble beasts;
With asses all his time he spent,
Their club's perpetual president.
He caught their manners, looks, and airs;
An ass in everything but ears!
If e'er his Highness meant a joke,
They grinn'd applause before he spoke;
But at each word what shouts of praise!
Good gods! how natural he brays!

Elate with flattery and conceit,
He seeks his royal sire's retreat;
Forward, and fond to show his parts,
His Highness brays; the Lion starts.
  "Puppy! that cursed vociferation
Betrays thy life and conversation:
Coxcombs, an ever-noisy race,
Are trumpets of their own disgrace."
  "Why so severe?" the Cub replies,
"Our senate always held me wise."
  "How weak is pride!" returns the sire;
"All fools are vain when fools admire!
But know, what stupid asses prize,
Lions and noble beasts despise."

FABLE 20

The Old Hen and the Cock

"Restrain your child!" you'll soon believe
 The text which says we sprung from Eve.
   As an old Hen led forth her train,
And seem'd to peck to show the grain,
She raked the chaff, she scratch'd the ground,
And glean'd the spacious yard around.
A giddy chick, to try her wings,
On the well's narrow margin springs,
And prone she drops. The mother's breast
All day with sorrow was possess'd.
   A Cock she met; her son she knew;
And in her heart affection grew.
   "My son," says she, "I grant your years
Have reach'd beyond a mother's cares;
I see you vigorous, strong, and bold;
I hear with joy your triumphs told.
'Tis not from Cocks thy fate I dread;
But let thy ever-wary tread
Avoid yon well; that fatal place
Is sure perdition to our race.
Print this my counsel on thy breast;
To the just gods I leave the rest."
   He thank'd her care; yet day by day
His bosom burn'd to disobey,
And every time the well he saw,
Scorn'd in his heart the foolish law:
         Near and more near each day he drew,

And long'd to try the dangerous view.
   "What was this idle charge?" he cries,
"Let courage female fears despise.
Or did she doubt my heart was brave,
And therefore this injunction gave?
Or does her harvest store the place,
A treasure for her younger race?
And would she thus my search prevent?
I stand resolved, and dare th' event."
   Thus said, he mounts the margin round,
And pries into the depths profound.
He stretch'd his neck, and from below,
With stretching neck, advanced a foe:
With wrath his ruffled plumes he rears,
The foe with ruffled plumes appears;
Threat answered threat, his fury grew,
Headlong to meet the war he flew,
But when the watery death he found,
He thus lamented as he drown'd;
   "I ne'er had been in this condition,
But for my mother's prohibition."

FABLE 21

The Ratcatcher and Cats

The rats by night such mischief did,
Betty was every morning chid.
They undermined whole sides of bacon,
Her cheese was sapp'd, her tarts were taken;
Her pasties, fenced with thickest paste,
Were all demolish'd and laid waste:
She cursed the Cat, for want of duty,
Who left her foes a constant booty.
   An engineer, of noted skill,
Engaged to stop the growing ill.
   From room to room he now surveys
Their haunts, their works, their secret ways;
Finds where they 'scape an ambuscade,
And whence the nightly sally's made.
   An envious Cat from place to place,
Unseen, attends his silent pace.
She saw that if his trade went on,
The purring race must be undone;
So secretly removes his baits,
And every stratagem defeats.
   Again he sets the poison'd toils,
And puss again the labour foils.
   "What foe, to frustrate my designs,
My schemes thus nightly countermines?"
Incensed, he cries; "this very hour
The wretch shall bleed beneath my power."
   So said, a pond'rous trap he brought,
And in the fact poor Puss was caught.
   "Smuggler," says he, "thou shalt be made
A victim to our loss of trade."
   The captive Cat, with piteous mews,
For pardon, life, and freedom sues:
   "A sister of the science spare;
One interest is our common care."
"What insolence!" the man replied;
"Shall Cats with us the game divide?

Were all your interloping band
Extinguish'd, or expell'd the land,
We ratcatchers might raise our fees,
Sole guardians of a nation's cheese!"
   A Cat, who saw the lifted knife,
Thus spoke, and saved her sister's life:
   "In every age and clime we see,
Two of a trade can ne'er agree.
Each hates his neighbour for encroaching;
'Squire stigmatizes 'squire for poaching;
Beauties with beauties are in arms,
And scandal pelts each other's charms;
Kings, too, their neighbour kings dethrone,
In hope to make the world their own:
But let us limit our desires,
   Not war like beauties, kings, and 'squires!
For though we both one prey pursue,
There's game enough for us and you."

FABLE 22

The Goat Without a Beard

"Tis certain that the modish passions
Descend among the crowd, like fashions.
Excuse me, then, if pride, conceit,
(The manners of the fair and great)
I give to monkeys, asses, dogs,
Fleas, owls, goats, butterflies, and hogs.
I say that these are proud, what then?
I never said they equal men.
A Goat (as vain as Goat can be)
Affected singularity;

Whene'er a thymy bank he found,
He roll'd upon the fragrant ground,
And then with fond attention stood,
Fix'd o'er his image in the flood.
　"I hate my frowzy beard," he cries,
"My youth is lost in this disguise.
Did not the females know my vigour,
Well might they loath this reverend figure."
　Resolved to smooth his shaggy face,
He sought the barber of the place.
A flippant monkey, spruce and smart,
Hard by, profess'd the dapper art.
His pole with pewter basins hung,
Black rotten teeth in order strung,
Ranged cups, that in the window stood,
Lined with red rags, to look like blood,
Did well his threefold trade explain,
Who shaved, drew teeth, and breathed a vein.
　The Goat he welcomes with an air,
And seats him in his wooden chair:
Mouth, nose, and cheek, the lather hides;
Light, smooth, and swift, the razor glides.
　"I hope your custom, Sir," says Pug,
"Sure never face was half so smug!"
The Goat, impatient for applause.
Swift to the neighbouring hill withdraws;
The shaggy people grinn'd and stared.
　"Heyday! what's here? without a beard!
Say, brother, whence the dire disgrace?
What envious hand hath robb'd your face?"
　When thus the fop with smiles of scorn:
"Are beards by civil nations worn?
Ev'n Muscovites have mow'd their chins.
Shall we, like formal Capuchins,
Stubborn in pride, retain the mode,
And bear about the hairy load?
Whene'er we through the village stray,
Are we not mock'd along the way,
Insulted with loud shouts of scorn,
By boys, our beards disgraced and torn?"
　"Were you no more with Goats to dwell,
Brother, I grant you reason well,"
Replies a bearded chief. "Beside,
If boys can mortify thy pride,
How wilt thou stand the ridicule
Of our whole flock? Affected fool!
Coxcombs, distinguish'd from the rest,
To all but coxcombs are a jest."

FABLE 23

The Old Woman and Her Cats

Who friendship with a knave hath made,
Is judged a partner in the trade.
The matron who conducts abroad
A willing nymph, is thought a bawd;
And if a modest girl is seen
With one who cures a lover's spleen,
We guess her not extremely nice,
And only wish to know her price.
'Tis thus that on the choice of friends
Our good or evil name depends.
　A wrinkled hag, of wicked fame,
Beside a little smoky flame
Sate hovering, pinch'd with age and frost;
Her shrivell'd hands, with veins emboss'd,
Upon her knees her weight sustains,
While palsy shook her crazy brains:
She mumbles forth her backward prayers,
An untamed scold of fourscore years:
About her swarm'd a numerous brood
Of Cats, who, lank with hunger, mew'd.
　Teased with their cries her choler grew,
And thus she sputter'd, "Hence, ye crew!
Fool that I was, to entertain
Such imps, such fiends, a hellish train!

Had ye been never housed and nursed,
I for a witch had ne'er been cursed.
To you I owe that crowds of boys
Worry me with eternal noise;
The horseshoe's nail'd (each threshold's guard);
Straws laid across, my pace retard,
The stunted broom the wenches hide,
For fear that I should up and ride;
They stick with pins my bleeding seat,
And bid me show my secret teat."
  "To hear you prate would vex a saint;
Who hath most reason of complaint?"
Replies a Cat: "Let's come to proof.
Had we ne'er starved beneath your roof,
We had, like others of our race,
In credit lived as beasts of chase.
'Tis infamy to serve a Hag;
Cats are thought imps, her broom a nag!
And boys against our lives combine,
Because, 'tis said, your Cats have nine."

FABLE 24

The Butterfly and the Snail

All upstarts, insolent in place,
 Remind us of their vulgar race.
  As in the sunshine of the morn,
A Butterfly, but newly born,
Sat proudly perking on a rose,
With pert conceit his bosom glows;
His wings, all glorious to behold,
Bedropt with azure, jet, and gold,
Wide he displays; the spangled dew
Reflects his eyes and various hue.
  His now-forgotten friend, a Snail,
Beneath his house, with slimy trail
Crawls o'er the grass, whom when he spies,
In wroth he to the gardener cries:

"What means yon peasant's daily toil,
From choking weeds to rid the soil?
Why wake you to the morning's care?
Why with new arts correct the year?
Why grows the peach with crimson hue?
And why the plum's inviting blue?
Were they to feast his taste design'd,
That vermin of voracious kind?
Crush then the slow, the pilfering race,
So purge thy garden from disgrace."
  "What arrogance!" the Snail replied.
"How insolent is upstart pride!
Hadst thou not thus, with insult vain,
Provoked my patience to complain,
I had conceal'd thy meaner birth,
Nor traced thee to the scum of earth:
For scarce nine suns have waked the hours,
To swell the fruit, and paint the flowers,
Since I thy humbler life survey'd,
In base, in sordid guise array'd.
A hideous insect, vile, unclean,
You dragged a slow and noisome train,
And from your spider-bowels drew
Foul film, and spun the dirty clue.
I own my humble life, good friend;
Snail was I born, and Snail shall end.
And, what's a Butterfly? At best,
He's but a caterpillar drest;
And all thy race, a numerous seed,
Shall prove of caterpillar breed."

FABLE 25

The Scold and the Parrot

The husband thus reproved his wife:
  "Who deals in slander, lives in strife.
Art thou the herald of disgrace,
Denouncing war to all thy race?
Can nothing quell thy thunder's rage,
Which spares nor friend, nor sex, nor age?
That vixen tongue of yours, my dear,
Alarms our neighbours far and near.
Good gods! 'tis like a rolling river,
That murmuring flows, and flows for ever!
Ne'er tired, perpetual discord sowing!
Like fame, it gathers strength by going."
  "Hey-day," the flippant tongue replies,
"How solemn is the fool! how wise!
Is Nature's choicest gift debarr'd?
Nay, frown not, for I will be heard.
Women of late are finely ridden,
A Parrot's privilege forbidden!
You praise his talk, his squalling song,
But wives are always in the wrong."
  Now reputations flew in pieces
Of mothers, daughters, aunts, and nieces:
She ran the Parrot's language o'er,
Bawd, hussy, drunkard, slattern, whore;
On all the sex she vents her fury,
Tries and condemns without a jury.
  At once the torrent of her words
Alarm'd cat, monkey, dogs, and birds;
All join their forces to confound her,
Puss spits, the monkey chatters round her;
The yelping cur her heels assaults:
The magpie blabs out all her faults;
Poll, in the uproar, from his cage,
With this rebuke outscream'd her rage:
  "A Parrot is for talking prized,

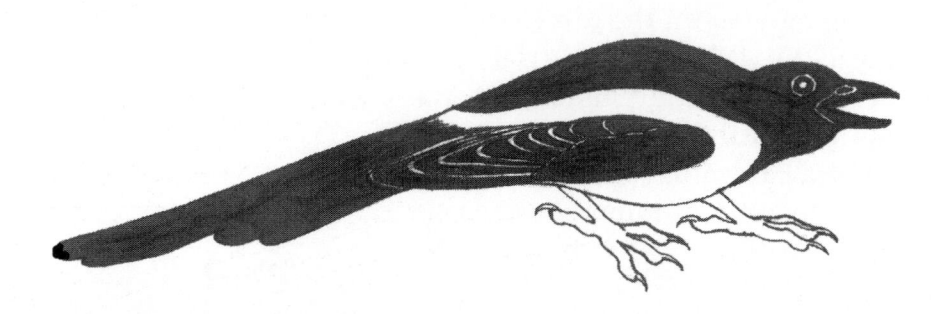

But prattling women are despised.
She who attacks another's honour,
Draws every living thing upon her:
Think, Madam, when you stretch your lungs,
That all your neighbours too have tongues.
One slander must ten thousand get;
The world with interest pays the debt."

FABLE 26

The Cur and the Mastiff

A sneaking Cur, the master's spy,
Rewarded for his daily lie,
With secret jealousies and fears
Set all together by the ears.

Poor puss to-day was in disgrace,
Another Cat supplied her place;
The hound was beat, the Mastiff chid,
The monkey was the room forbid.
Each to his dearest friend grew shy,
And none could tell the reason why.
　A plan to rob the house was laid:
The thief with love seduced the maid,
Cajol'd the Cur, and stroked his head,
And bought his secrecy with bread.
He next the Mastiff's honour tried,
Whose honest jaws the bribe defied:
He stretch'd his hand to proffer more;
The surly Dog his fingers tore.
　Swift ran the Cur; with indignation
The master took his information.
"Hang him, the villain's cursed," he cries;
And round his neck the halter ties.
　The Dog his humble suit preferr'd
And begg'd in justice to be heard.
The master sat. On either hand
The cited Dogs confronting stand;
The Cur the bloody tales relates,
And like a lawyer, aggravates.
　"Judge not unheard," the Mastiff cried,
"But weigh the cause of either side.
Think not that treachery can be just,
Take not informers' words on trust.
They ope their hand to every pay,
And you and me by turns betray."
　He spoke; and all the truth appear'd;
The Cur was hang'd, the Mastiff clear'd.

FABLE 27

The Sick Man and the Angel

"Is there no hope?" the sick man said.
The silent doctor shook his head,
And took his leave with signs of sorrow,
Despairing of his fee to-morrow.
    When thus the Man, with gasping breath;
"I feel the chilling wound of Death!
Since I must bid the world adieu,

Let me my former life review.
I grant, my bargains well were made,
But all men over-reach in trade:
'Tis self-defence in each profession;
Sure self-defence is no transgression.
The little portion in my hands,
By good security on lands
Is well increased. If, unawares,
My justice to myself and heirs
Hath let my debtor rot in jail,
For want of good sufficient bail;
If I by writ, or bond, or deed,
Reduced a family to need,
My will hath made the world amends;
My hope on charity depends.
When I am number'd with the dead,
And all my pious gifts are read,
By heaven and earth 'twill then be known
My charities were amply shown."
 An Angel came: "Ah! friend," he cried,
"No more in flattering hope confide.
Can thy good deeds in former times
Outweigh the balance of thy crimes?
What widow or what orphan prays
To crown thy life with length of days?
A pious action's in thy power,
Embrace with joy the happy hour.
Now while you draw the vital air,
Prove your intention is sincere:
This instant give a hundred pound;
Your neighbours want, and you abound."
 "But why such haste," the sick Man whines:
"Who knows as yet what Heaven designs?
Perhaps I may recover still;
That sum and more are in my will."
 "Fool," says the Vision, "now 'tis plain
Your life, your soul, your heaven, was gain.
From every side, with all your might,
You scraped, and scraped beyond your right;
And after death would fain atone,
By giving what is not your own."
 "While there is life, there's hope," he cried,
Then why such haste?" so groan'd and died.

FABLE 28

The Persian, the Sun, and the Cloud

Is there a bard whom genius fires,
Whose ev'ry thought the god inspires?
When Envy reads the nervous lines,
She frets, she rails, she raves, she pines;
Her hissing snakes with venom swell;
She calls her venal train from hell:
The servile fiends her nod obey,
And all Curll's authors are in pay.
Fame calls up Calumny and Spite;
Thus shadow owes its birth to light.
   As prostrate to the god of day,
With heart devout, a Persian lay,
His invocation thus begun:
   "Parent of light! all seeing Sun!
Prolific beam, whose rays dispense
The various gifts of Providence;
Accept our praise, our daily prayer,
Smile on our fields, and bless the year."
   A Cloud, who mock'd his grateful tongue,
The day with sudden darkness hung;
With pride and envy swell'd, aloud
A voice thus thunder'd from the Cloud:
   "Weak is this gaudy god of thine,
Whom I at will, forbid to shine.
Shall I nor vows nor incense know?
Where praise is due, the praise bestow."
With fervent zeal the Persian moved,
Thus the proud calumny reproved:
   "It was that god who claims my prayer,
Who gave thee birth, and raised thee there;
When o'er his beams the veil is thrown,
Thy substance is but plainer shown:

A passing gale, a puff of wind,
Dispels thy thickest troops combined."
 The gale arose; the vapour tost
(The sport of winds) in air was lost;
The glorious orb the day refines:
Thus Envy breaks, thus Merit shines.

FABLE 29

The Fox at the Point of Death

A Fox, in life's extreme decay,
Weak, sick, and faint, expiring lay;
All appetite had left his maw,
And age disarm'd his mumbling jaw.
His numerous race around him stand,
To learn their dying sire's command:
He raised his head with whining moan,
And thus was heard the feeble tone:
  "Ah, sons! from evil ways depart;
My crimes lie heavy on my heart.
See, see the murder'd geese appear!
Why are those bleeding turkeys there?
Why all around this cackling train,
Who haunt my ears for chickens slain?"
  The hungry Foxes round them stared,
And for the promised feast prepared.
  "Where, Sir, is all this dainty cheer?
Nor turkey, goose, nor hen, is here:
These are the phantoms of your brain,
And your sons lick their lips in vain."
  "O gluttons!" says the drooping sire,
"Restrain inordinate desire:
Your liquorish taste you shall deplore,
When peace of conscience is no more.

Does not the hound betray our pace,
And gins and guns destroy our race?
Thieves dread the searching eye of power,
And never feel the quiet hour.
Old age (which few of us shall know)
Now puts a period to my woe.
Would you true happiness attain,
Let honesty your passions rein;
So live in credit and esteem,
And the good name you lost, redeem."

  "The counsel's good," a Fox replies,
"Could we perform what you advise.
Think what our ancestors have done?
A line of thieves from son to son:
To us descends the long disgrace,
And infamy hath mark'd our race.
Though we, like harmless sheep, should feed,
Honest in thought, in word, and deed;
Whatever hen-roost is decreased,
We shall be thought to share the feast.
The change shall never be believed:
A lost good name is ne'er retrieved."

  "Nay, then," replies the feeble Fox,
But hark! I hear a hen that clocks
Go, but be moderate in your food:
A chicken, too, might do me good."

FABLE 30

The Setting Dog and the Partridge

The ranging Dog the stubble tries,
And searches every breeze that flies.
The scent grows warm; with cautious fear
He creeps, and points the covey near;
The men in silence, far behind,
Conscious of game the net unbind.
   A Partridge, with experience wise,
The fraudful preparation spies;
She mocks their toils, alarms her brood,
The covey springs, and seeks the wood;
But, ere her certain wing she tries,
Thus to the creeping Spaniel cries:

"Thou fawning slave to man's deceit,
Thou pimp of luxury, sneaking cheat,
Of thy whole species, thou disgrace,
Dogs should disown thee of their race!
For if I judge their native parts,
They're born with honest, open hearts;
And, ere they served man's wicked ends,
Were generous foes, or real friends."
  When thus the dog, with scornful smile:
"Secure of wing, thou dar'st revile.
Clowns are to polish'd manners blind:
How ign'rant is the rustic mind!
My worth sagacious courtiers see,
And to preferment rise like me.
The thriving pimp, who beauty sets,
Hath oft enhanced a nation's debts;
Friend sets his friend, without regard,
And ministers his skill reward:
Thus train'd by man, I learnt his ways,
And growing favour feasts my days."
  "I might have guess'd," the Partridge said,
"The place where you were train'd and fed;
Servants are apt, and in a trice
Ape to a hair their master's vice.
You came from court, you say-Adieu,"
She said, and to the covey flew.

FABLE 31

The Universal Apparition

A Rake, by every passion ruled,
 With every vice his youth had cool'd;
Disease his tainted blood assails,
His spirits droop, his vigour fails
With secret ills at home he pines,
And, like infirm old age, declines.
As twinged with pain, he pensive sits,
And raves, and prays, and swears, by fits:
A ghastly phantom, lean and wan,
Before him rose, and thus began
　"My name, perhaps, hath reached your ear;
Attend, and be advised by Care.
Nor love, nor honour, wealth, nor pow'r,
Can give the heart a cheerful hour
When health is lost. Be timely wise:
With health all taste of pleasure flies."
　Thus said, the phantom disappears.
The wary counsel waked his fears:
He now from all excess abstains,
With physic purifies his veins;
And, to procure a sober life,
Resolves to venture on a wife.
　But now again the Sprite ascends,
Where'er he walks his ear attends;
Insinuates that beauty's frail,
That perseverance must prevail;
With jealousies his brain inflames,
And whispers all her lovers' names.

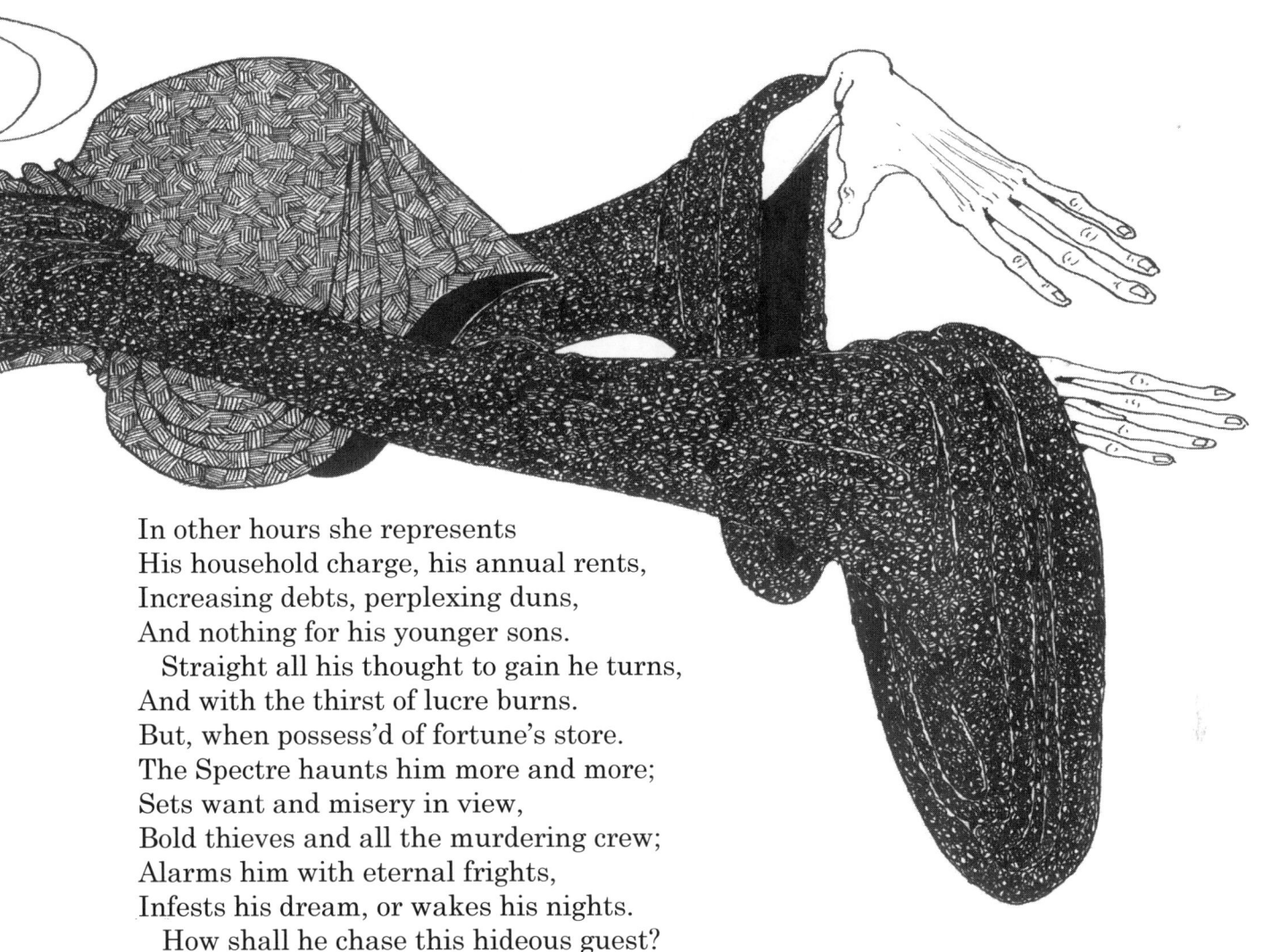

In other hours she represents
His household charge, his annual rents,
Increasing debts, perplexing duns,
And nothing for his younger sons.
   Straight all his thought to gain he turns,
And with the thirst of lucre burns.
But, when possess'd of fortune's store.
The Spectre haunts him more and more;
Sets want and misery in view,
Bold thieves and all the murdering crew;
Alarms him with eternal frights,
Infests his dream, or wakes his nights.
   How shall he chase this hideous guest?
Power may perhaps protect his rest.
To power he rose. Again the Sprite
Besets him, morning, noon, and night;
Talks of Ambition's tottering seat,
How Envy persecutes the great;
Of rival hate, of treach'rous friends,
And what disgrace his fall attends.
   The court he quits to fly from Care,
And seeks the peace of rural air:
His groves, his fields, amused his hours;
He pruned his trees, he raised his flowers.
But Care again his steps pursues,
Warns him of blasts, of blighting dews,
Of plundering insects, snails, and rains,
And droughts that starved the labour'd plains.
Abroad, at home, the Spectre's there;
In vain we seek to fly from Care.
At length he thus the Ghost addrest:
"Since thou must be my constant guest
Be kind, and follow me no more;
For Care, by right, should go before."

FABLE 32

The Two Owls and the Sparrow

Two formal Owls together sat,
Conferring thus in solemn chat:
  "How is the modern taste decay'd!
Where's the respect to wisdom paid?
Our worth the Grecian sages knew;
They gave our sires the honour due;
They weigh'd the dignity of fowls,
And pry'd into the depth of Owls.
Athens, the seat of learned fame,
With general voice revered our name;
On merit title was conferr'd,
And all adored th' Athenian bird."
  "Brother, you reason well," replies
The solemn mate, with half-shut eyes;
"Right: Athens was the seat of learning;
And truly wisdom is discerning.
Besides, on Pallas' helm we sit?
The type and ornament of wit:
But now, alas! we're quite neglected,
And a pert Sparrow's more respected."
  A Sparrow, who was lodged beside,
O'erhears them soothe each other's pride,
And thus he nimbly vents his heat:
  "Who meets a fool must find conceit.
I grant you were at Athens graced,
And on Minerva's helm were placed;
But every bird that wings the sky,
Except an Owl, can tell you why.
From hence they taught their schools to know
How false we judge by outward show;
That we should never looks esteem,
Since fools as wise as you, might seem.

Would ye contempt and scorn avoid,
Let your vainglory be destroy'd;
Humble your arrogance of thought,
Pursue the ways by nature taught;
So shall you find delicious fare,
And grateful farmers praise your care;
So shall sleek mice your chase reward,
And no keen cat find more regard."

FABLE 33

The Courtier and Proteus

Whene'er a Courtier's out of place,
The country shelters his disgrace;
Where, doom'd to exercise and health,
His house and gardens own his wealth.
He builds new schemes, in hope to gain
The plunder of another reign;
Like Philip's son, would fain be doing,
And sighs for other realms to ruin.

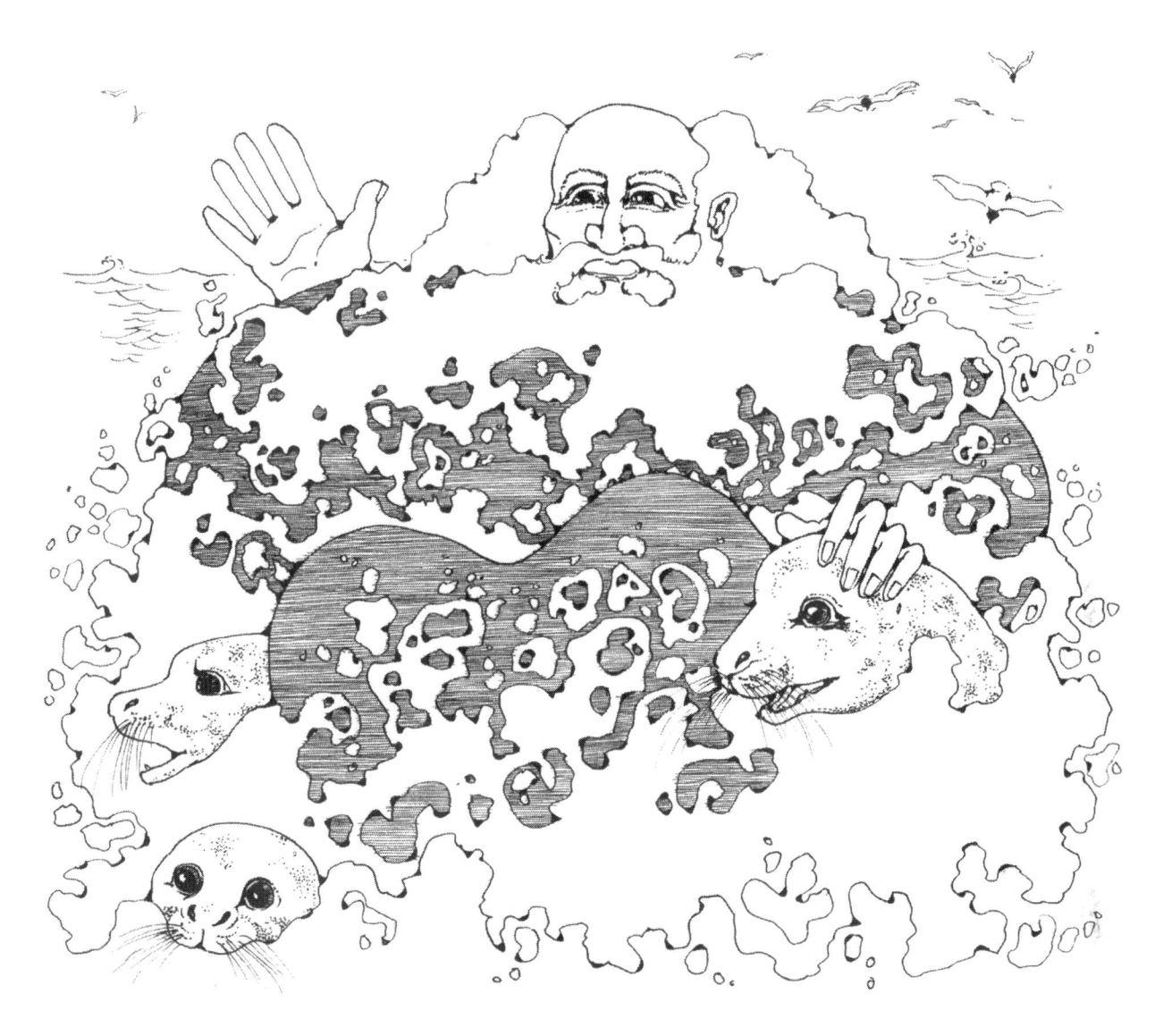

As one of these (without his wand),
Pensive along the winding strand
Employ'd the solitary hour,
In projects to regain his power,
The waves in spreading circles ran,
Proteus arose, and thus began:
"Came you from court? for in your mien
A self-important air is seen."
He frankly own'd his friends had trick'd him,
And how he fell his party's victim.
"Know," says the god, "by matchless skill
I change to every shape at will;
But yet I'm told, at court you see
Those who presume to rival me."

Thus said: a snake, with hideous trail,
Proteus extends his scaly mail.
    "Know," says the man, "though proud in place,
All courtiers are of reptile race.
Like you, they take that dreadful form,
Bask in the sun, and fly the storm;
With malice hiss, with envy gloat,
And for convenience change their coat:
With new-got lustre rear their head,
Though on a dunghill born and bred."
    Sudden the god a lion stands;
He shakes his mane, he spurns the sands;
Now a fierce lynx, with fiery glare;
A wolf, an ass, a fox, a bear.

"Had I ne'er lived at court," he cries,
"Such transformation might surprise;
But there, in quest of daily game,
Each able Courtier acts the same.
Wolves, lions, lynxes, while in place,
Their friends and fellows are their chase.
They play the bear's and fox's part,
Now rob by force, now steal with art.
They sometimes in the senate bray,
Or, changed again to beasts of prey,
Down from the lion to the ape,
Practise the frauds of every shape."
  So said, upon the god he flies,
In cords the struggling captive ties.
  "Now, Proteus! now (to truth compell'd)
Speak, and confess thy art excell'd.
Use strength, surprise, or what you will,
The Courtier finds evasions still;
Not to be bound by any ties,
And never forced to leave his lies."

FABLE 34

The Mastiff

Those who in quarrels interpose,
Must often wipe a bloody nose.
A Mastiff of true English blood,
Loved fighting better than his food,
When dogs were snarling for a bone,
He long'd to make the war his own,
And often found (when two contend)
To interpose obtain'd his end.
He gloried in his limping pace;
The scars of honour seamed his face,
In every limb a gash appears,
And frequent fights retrench'd his ears.
   As, on a time, he heard from far
Two dogs engaged in noisy war,
Away he scours, and lays about him,
Resolved no fray should be without him.
   Forth from his yard a tanner flies,
And to the bold intruder cries:
"A cudgel shall correct your manners:
Whence sprung this cursed hate to tanners?
While on my dog you vent your spite,
Sirrah! 'tis me you dare not bite."
   To see the battle thus perplex'd,
With equal rage a butcher vex'd,
Hoarse-screaming from the circled crowd,
To the cursed Mastiff cries aloud,
   "Both Hockley-hole and Mary-bone'
The combats of my dog have known:
He ne'er, like bullies, coward-hearted,
Attacks in public to be parted.
Think not, rash fool, to share his fame;
Be his the honour or the shame."
   Thus said, they swore, and raved like thunder,
Then dragg'd their fasten'd dogs asunder;
While club and kicks from ev'ry side
Rebounded from the Mastiff's hide.
   All reeking now with sweat and blood,
Awhile the parted warriors stood;
Then pour'd upon the meddling foe,
Who, worried, howl'd, and sprawl'd below.
He rose; and, limping from the fray,
By both sides mangled, sneak'd away.

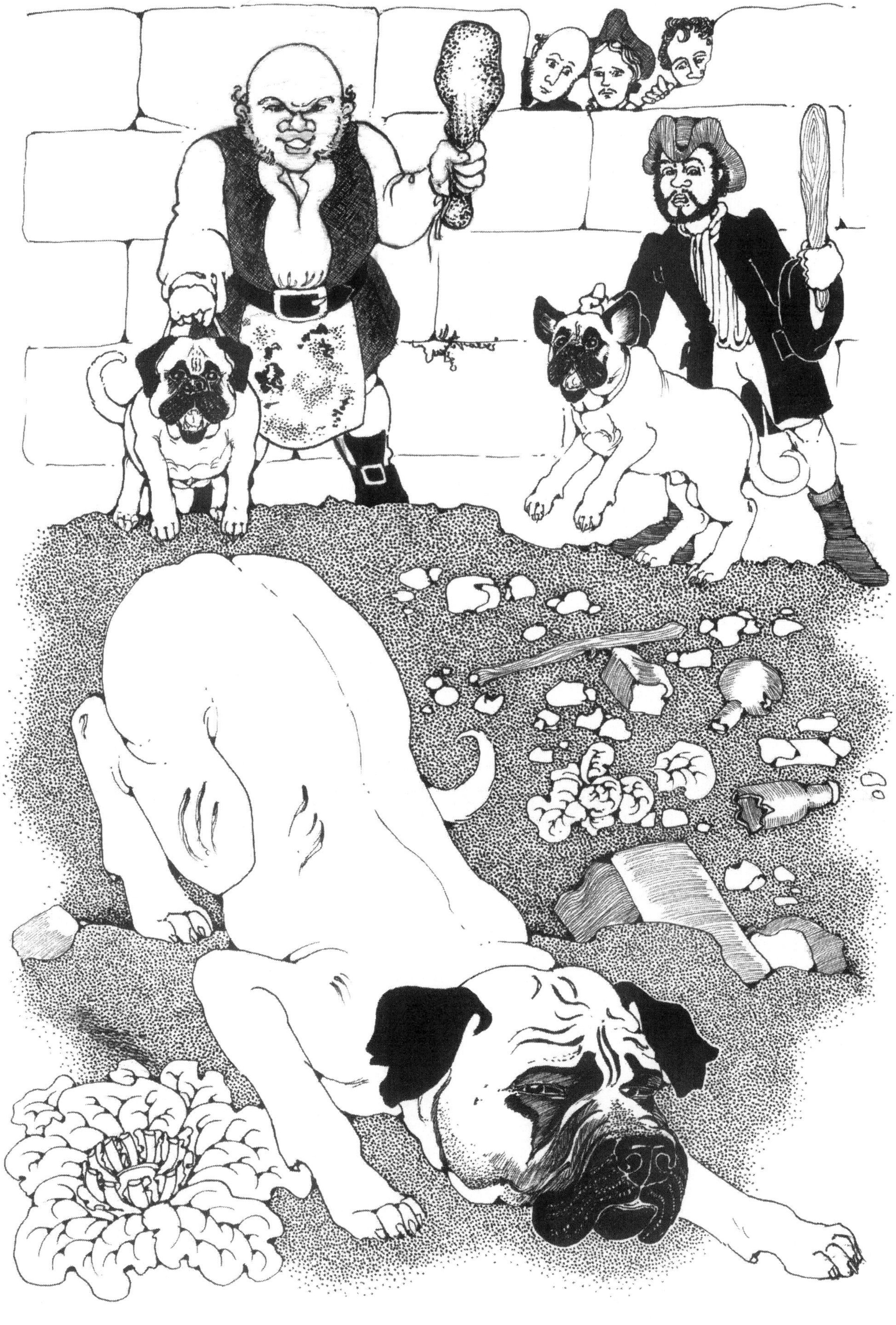

FABLE 35

The Barley-Mow and the Dunghill

How many saucy airs we meet
From Temple Bar to Aldgate Street!
Proud rogues, who shared the South-sea prey,
And sprung, like mushrooms, in a day!

They think it mean to condescend
To know a brother or a friend;
They blush to hear their mother's name,
And by their pride expose their shame.

   As cross his yard, at early day,
A careful farmer took his way,
He stopp'd, and, leaning on his fork,
Observed the flail's incessant work.
In thought he measured all his store,
His geese, his hogs, he numbered o'er;
In fancy weigh'd the fleeces shorn,
And multiplied the next year's corn.

   A Barley-mow, which stood beside,
Thus to its musing master cried:
"Say, good sir, is it fit or right
To treat me with neglect and slight?
Me, who contribute to your cheer,
And raise your mirth with ale and beer?
Why thus insulted, thus disgraced,
And that vile Dunghill near me placed?
Are those poor sweepings of a groom,
That filthy sight, that nauseous fume,
Meet objects here? Command it hence;
A thing so mean must give offence."

   The humble Dunghill thus replied:
"Thy master hears, and mocks thy pride;
Insult not thus the meek and low;
In me thy benefactor know;
My warm assistance gave thee birth,
Or thou hadst perish'd low in earth;
But upstarts, to support their station,
Cancel at once all obligation."

FABLE 36

Pythagoras and the Countryman

Pythag'ras rose at early dawn
By soaring meditation drawn,
To breathe the fragrance of the day,
Through flowery fields he took his way.
His steps misled him to a farm,
Where on a ladder's topmost round,
A peasant stood; the hammer's sound
Shook the weak barn. "Say, Friend, what care
Calls for thy honest labour there?"
   The Clown, with surly voice, replies,
"Vengeance aloud for justice cries.
This kite, by daily rapine fed,
My hens' annoy, my turkeys' dread,
At length his forfeit life has paid;
See on the wall his wings display'd.
Here nail'd, a terror to his kind,
My fowls shall future safety find;
My yard the thriving poultry feed,
And my barn's refuse fat the breed."
   "Friend," says the Sage, "the doom is wise;
For public good the murderer dies
But if these tyrants of the air
Demand a sentence so severe,
Think how the glutton, man, devours;
What bloody feasts regale his hours!
O impudence of power and might,
Thus to condemn a hawk or kite,
When thou, perhaps, carniv'rous sinner,
Hadst pullets yesterday for dinner!"
   "Hold," cried the Clown, with passion heated,
Shall kites and men alike be treated?
When Heaven the world with creatures stored,
Man was ordain'd their sovereign lord."
   "Thus tyrants boast," the Sage replied,
"Whose murders spring from power and pride.
Own then this manlike kite is slain
Thy greater luxury to sustain;
For 'petty rogues submit to Fate,
That great ones may enjoy their state.'"

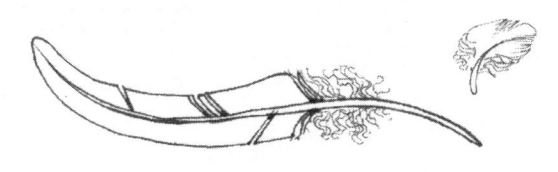

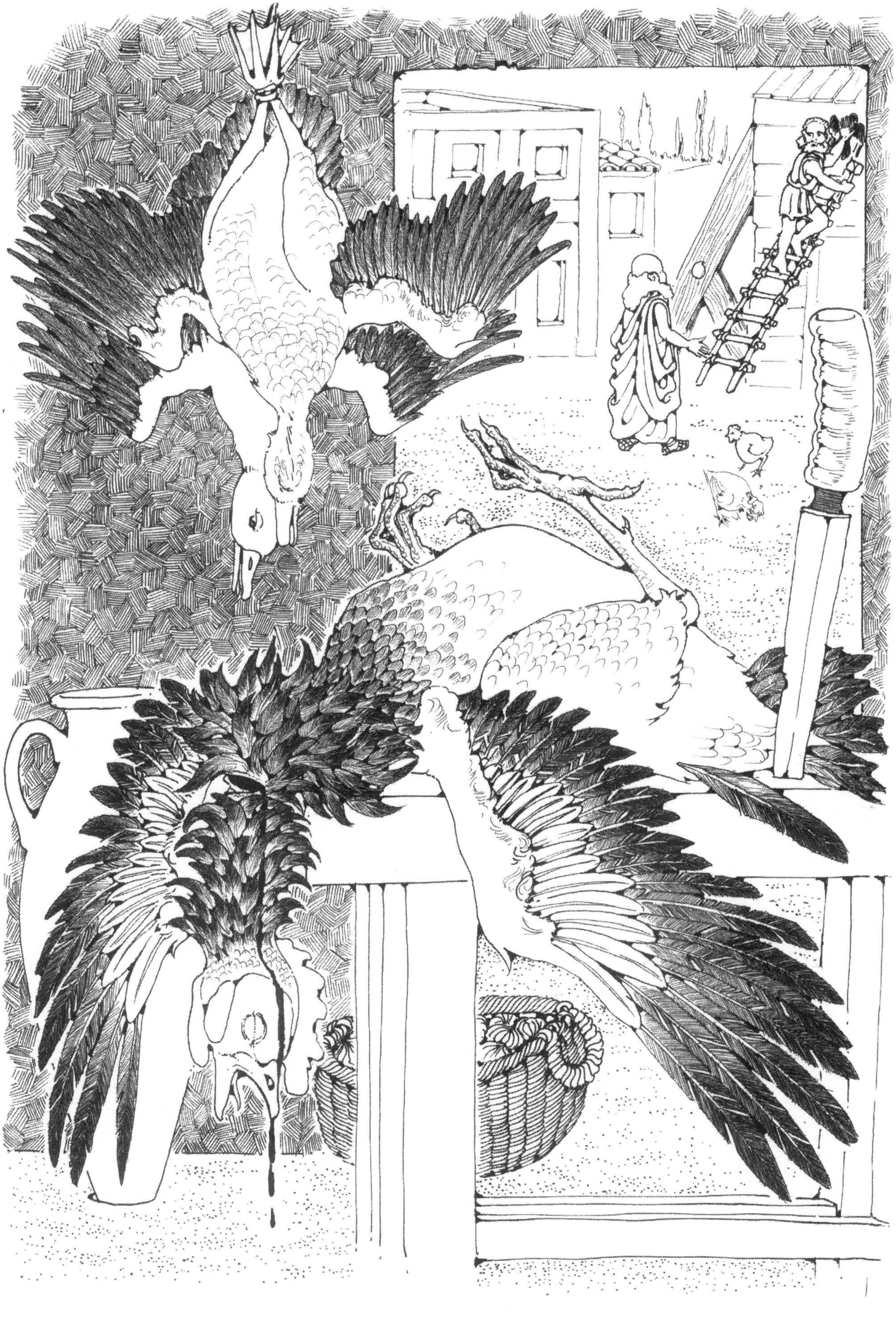

FABLE 37

The Farmer's Wife and the Raven

"Why are those tears? Why droops your head?
Is then your other husband dead?
Or does a worse disgrace betide!
Hath no one since his death applied?"
 "Alas! you know the cause too well;
The salt is spilt, to me it fell:
Then, to contribute to my loss,
My knife and fork were laid across;
On Friday, too! the day I dread!
Would I were safe at home in bed;
Last night (I vow to Heaven 'tis true)
Bounce from the fire a coffin flew,
Next post some fatal news shall tell;
God send my Cornish friends be well!"
 "Unhappy Widow, cease thy tears,
Nor feel affliction in thy fears;
Let not thy stomach be suspended;
Eat now, and weep when dinner's ended:

And when the butler clears the table,
For thy dessert, I'll read my Fable."
  Betwixt her swagging pannier's load
A Farmer's Wife to market rode,
And, jogging on, with thoughtful care,
Summ'd up the profits of her ware;
When, starting from her silver dream,
Thus far and wide was heard her scream:
  "That raven on yon left-hand oak
(Curse on his ill-betiding croak!)
Bodes me no good." No more she said,
When poor blind Ball, with stumbling tread,
Fell prone; o'erturned the pannier lay,
And her mash'd eggs bestrow'd the way.
  She, sprawling in the yellow road,
Rail'd, swore, and cursed: "Thou croaking toad,
A murrain take thy whoreson throat!
I knew misfortune in the note."
  "Dame," quoth the Raven, "spare your oaths,
Unclench your fist, and wipe your clothes.
But why on me those curses thrown?
Goody, the fault was all your own;
For had you laid this brittle ware
On Dun, the old sure-footed mare,
Though all the Ravens of the Hundred
With croaking had your tongue out-thunder'd,
Surefooted Dun had kept her legs,
And you, good woman, saved your eggs."

FABLE 38

The Turkey and the Ant

In other men we faults can spy,
And blame the mote that dims their eye;
Each little speck and blemish find,
To our own stronger errors blind.
   A Turkey, tired of common food,
Forsook the barn, and sought the wood;
Behind her ran an infant train,
Collecting here and there, a grain.

"Draw near, my birds!" the mother cries,
"This hill delicious fare supplies.
Behold the busy negro race;
See millions blacken all the place
Fear not; like me with freedom eat:
An Ant is most delightful meat.
How bless'd, how envied, were our life,
Could we but 'scape the poulterer's knife
But man, curs'd man, on Turkey preys,
And Christmas shortens all our days.
Sometimes with oysters we combine,
Sometimes assist the savoury chine.
From the low peasant to the lord,
The Turkey smokes on every board.
Sure men for gluttony are curs'd,
Of the seven deadly sins, the worst."
   An Ant, who climb'd beyond her reach,
Thus answer'd from the neighb'ring beech:
"Ere you remark another's sin,
Bid thy own conscience look within;
Control thy more voracious bill,
Nor, for a breakfast, nations kill."

FABLE 39

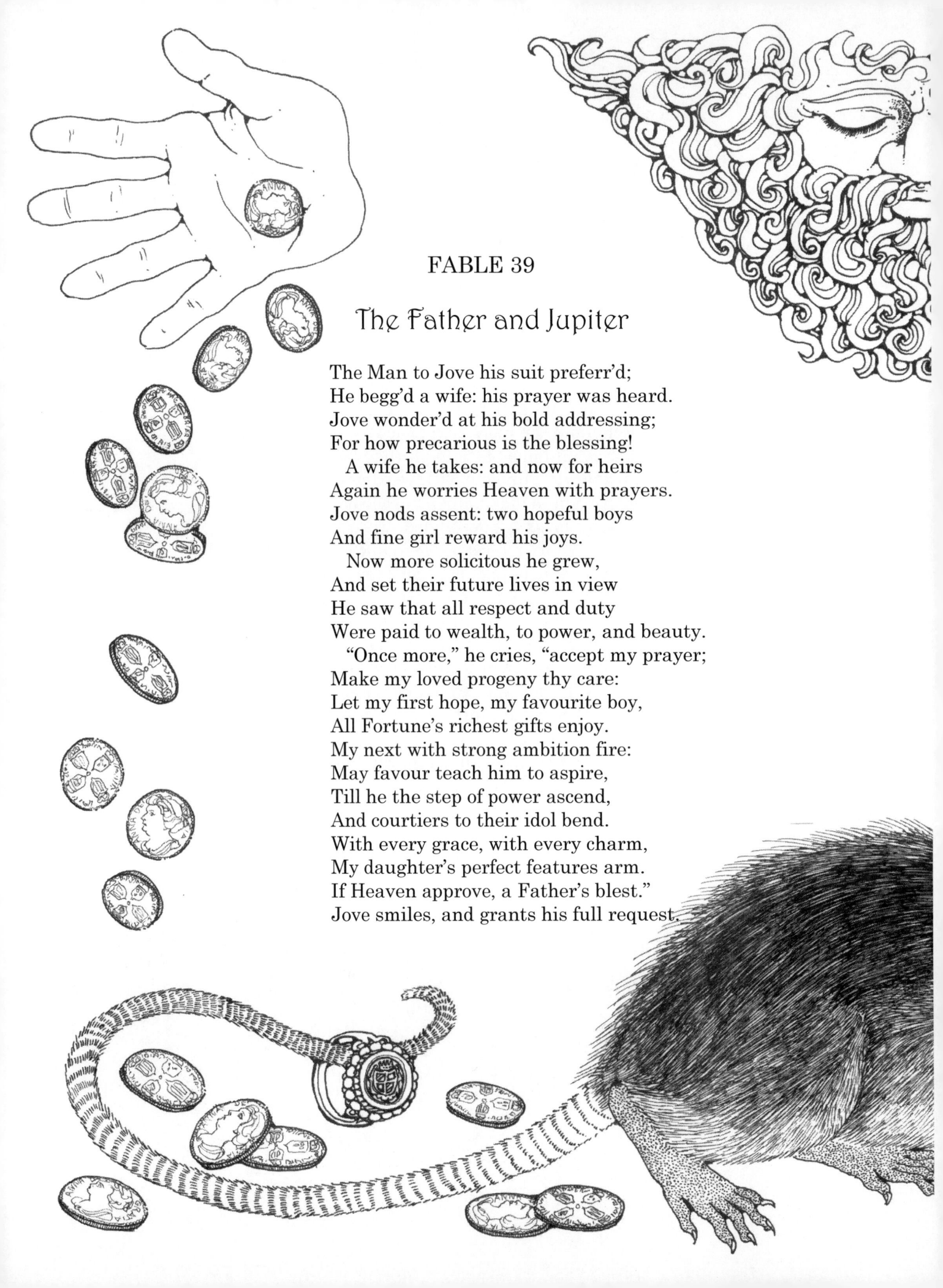

The Father and Jupiter

The Man to Jove his suit preferr'd;
He begg'd a wife: his prayer was heard.
Jove wonder'd at his bold addressing;
For how precarious is the blessing!
  A wife he takes: and now for heirs
Again he worries Heaven with prayers.
Jove nods assent: two hopeful boys
And fine girl reward his joys.
  Now more solicitous he grew,
And set their future lives in view
He saw that all respect and duty
Were paid to wealth, to power, and beauty.
  "Once more," he cries, "accept my prayer;
Make my loved progeny thy care:
Let my first hope, my favourite boy,
All Fortune's richest gifts enjoy.
My next with strong ambition fire:
May favour teach him to aspire,
Till he the step of power ascend,
And courtiers to their idol bend.
With every grace, with every charm,
My daughter's perfect features arm.
If Heaven approve, a Father's blest."
Jove smiles, and grants his full request.

The first, a miser at the heart,
Studious of every griping art,
Heaps hoards on hoards with anxious pain,
And all his life devotes to gain.
He feels no joy, his cares increase,
He neither wakes, nor sleeps, in peace;
In fancied want (a wretch complete)
He starves, and yet he dares not eat.
The next to sudden honours grew;
The thriving art of courts he knew;
He reach'd the height of power and place,
Then fell, the victim of disgrace.
    Beauty with early bloom supplies
His daughter's cheek and points her eyes.
The vain coquette each suit disdains,
And glories in her lovers' pains.
With age she fades, each lover flies:
Contemn'd, forlorn, she pines and dies.
When Jove the Father's grief survey'd,
And heard him Heaven and Fate upbraid,
Thus spoke the god: "By outward show,
Men judge of happiness and woe:
Shall ignorance of good and ill
Dare to direct th' eternal will?
Seek virtue: and, of that possess'd,
To Providence resign the rest."

FABLE 40

The Two Monkeys

The learned, full of inward pride,
The fops of outward show deride;
The fop, with learning at defiance,
Scoffs at the pedant and the science;
The Don, a formal solemn strutter,
Despises Monsieur's airs and flutter;
While Monsieur mocks the formal fool,
Who looks, and speaks, and walks, by rule.
Britain, a medley of the twain,
As pert as France, as grave as Spain,
In fancy wiser than the rest,
Laughs at them both, of both the jest,
Is not the Poet's chiming close,
Censured by all the sons of Prose?
While bards of quick imagination
Despise the sleepy prose narration.
Men laugh at apes, they men contemn;
For what are we, but apes to them?
  Two Monkeys went to Southwark fair,
No critics had a sourer air:
They forced their way through draggled folks,
Who gaped to catch Jack Pudding's jokes;
Then took their tickets for the show,
And got by chance the foremost row.
  To see their grave observing face
Provok'd a laugh throughout the place.
  "Brother," says Pug, and turn'd his head,
The rabble's monstrously ill-bred."
  Now through the booth loud hisses ran,
Nor ended till the show began.
  The tumbler whirls the flip-flap round,
With somersets he shakes the ground;
The cord beneath the dancer springs;
Aloft in air the vaulter swings;
Distorted now, now prone depends,
Now through his twisted arms ascends;

The crowd, in wonder and delight,
With clapping hands applaud the sight.
   With smiles, quoth pug, "If pranks like these
The giant apes of reason please,
How would they wonder at our arts?
They must adore us for our parts.
High on the twig I've seen you cling,
Play, twist, and turn in airy ring:
How can those clumsy things like me,
Fly with a bound from tree to tree?
But yet, by this applause, we find
These emulators of our kind
Discern our worth, our parts regard,
Who our mean mimics thus reward."
   "Brother," the grinning mate replies,
"In this I grant that Man is wise,
While good example they pursue,
We must allow some praise is due
But when they strain beyond their guide,
I laugh to scorn the mimic pride.
For how fantastic is the sight,
To meet men always bolt upright,
Because we sometimes walk on two!
I hate the imitating crew."

FABLE 41

The Owl and the Farmer

An Owl of grave deport and mien,
 Who (like the Turk) was seldom seen,
Within a barn had chose his station,
As fit for prey and contemplation.
Upon a beam aloft he sits,
And nods, and seems to think, by fits.
(So have I seen a man of news,
Or 'Post-boy' or 'Gazette' peruse,
Smoke, nod, and talk with voice profound,
And fix the fate of Europe round.)

Sheaves piled on sheaves, hid all the floor,
At dawn of morn to view his store
The Farmer came. The hooting guest,
His self-importance, thus exprest:
   "Reason in man is mere pretence:
How weak how shallow, is his sense!
To treat with scorn the Bird of Night,
Declares his folly or his spite.
Then, too, how partial is his praise!
The lark's, the linnet's chirping lays,
To his ill-judging ears are fine,
And nightingales are all divine:
But the more knowing feather'd race
See wisdom stamp'd upon my face
Whene'er to visit light I deign,
What flocks of fowl compose my train!
Like slaves, they crowd my flight behind,
And own me of superior kind."
   The Farmer laugh'd and thus replied:
"Thou dull important lump of pride,
Dars't thou with that harsh grating tongue
Depreciate birds of warbling song?
Indulge thy spleen. Know, men and fowl
Regard thee, as thou art, an owl,
Besides, proud Blockhead be not vain
Of what thou call'st thy slaves and train:
Few follow Wisdom or her rules;
Fools in derision follow fools."

FABLE 42

The Jugglers

A Juggler long through all the town
Had raised his fortune and renown;
You'd think (so far his art transcends)
The devil at his fingers' ends.
   Vice heard his fame, she read his bill;
Convinced of his inferior skill,
She sought his booth, and from the crowd
Defied the man of art aloud.
   "Is this then he so famed for sleight?
Can this slow bungler cheat your sight?
Dares he with me dispute the prize?
I leave it to impartial eyes."
   Provoked, the Juggler cried, "'Tis done;
In science I submit to none."
   Thus said, the cups and balls he play'd;
By turns this here, that there, convey'd.
The cards, obedient to his words,
Are by a fillip turn'd to birds.
His little boxes change the grain:
Trick after trick deludes the train.
He shakes his bag, he shows all fair;
His fingers spread, and nothing there:
Then bids it rain with showers of gold;
And now his ivory eggs are told!
But when from thence the hen he draws,
Amazed spectators hum applause.

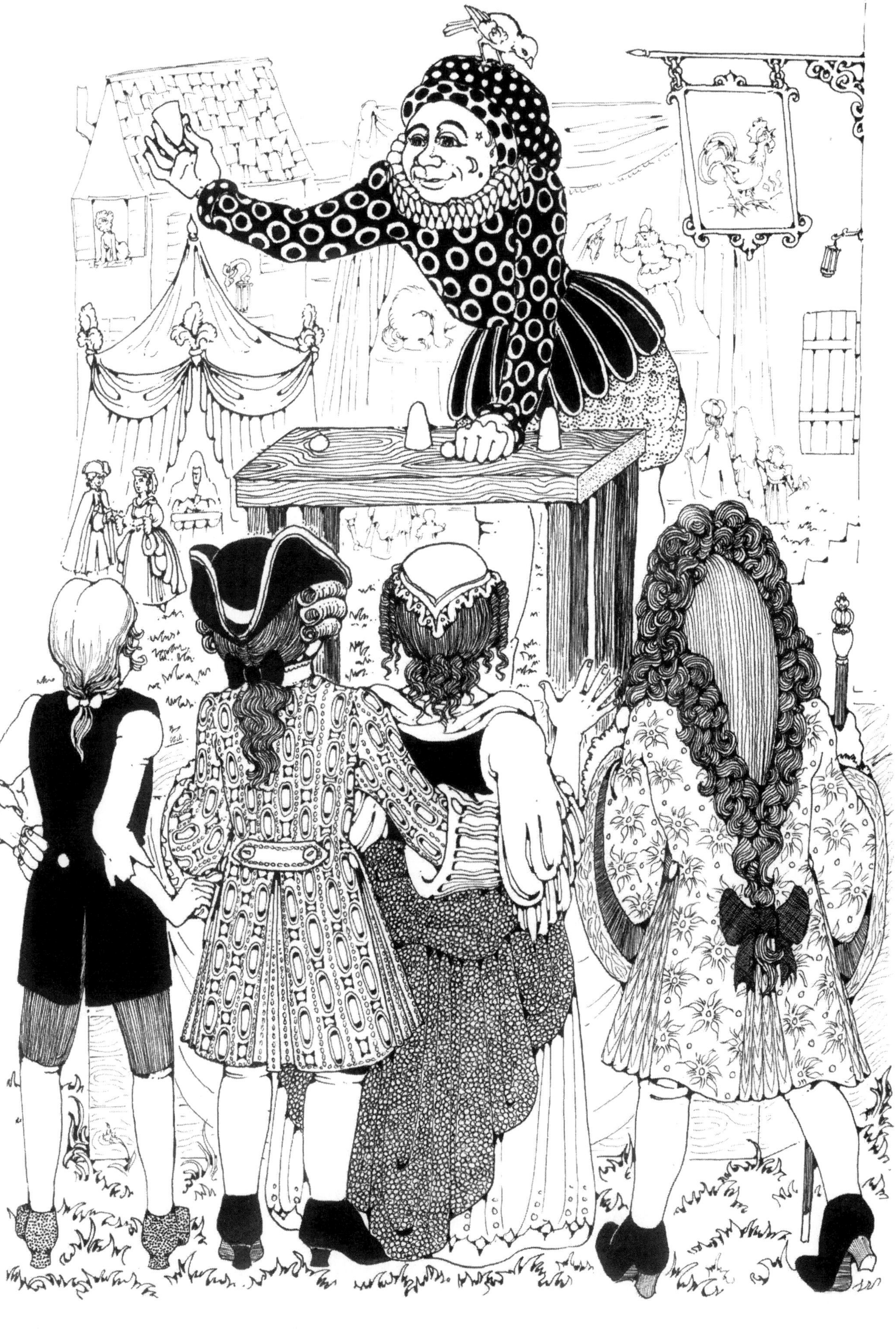

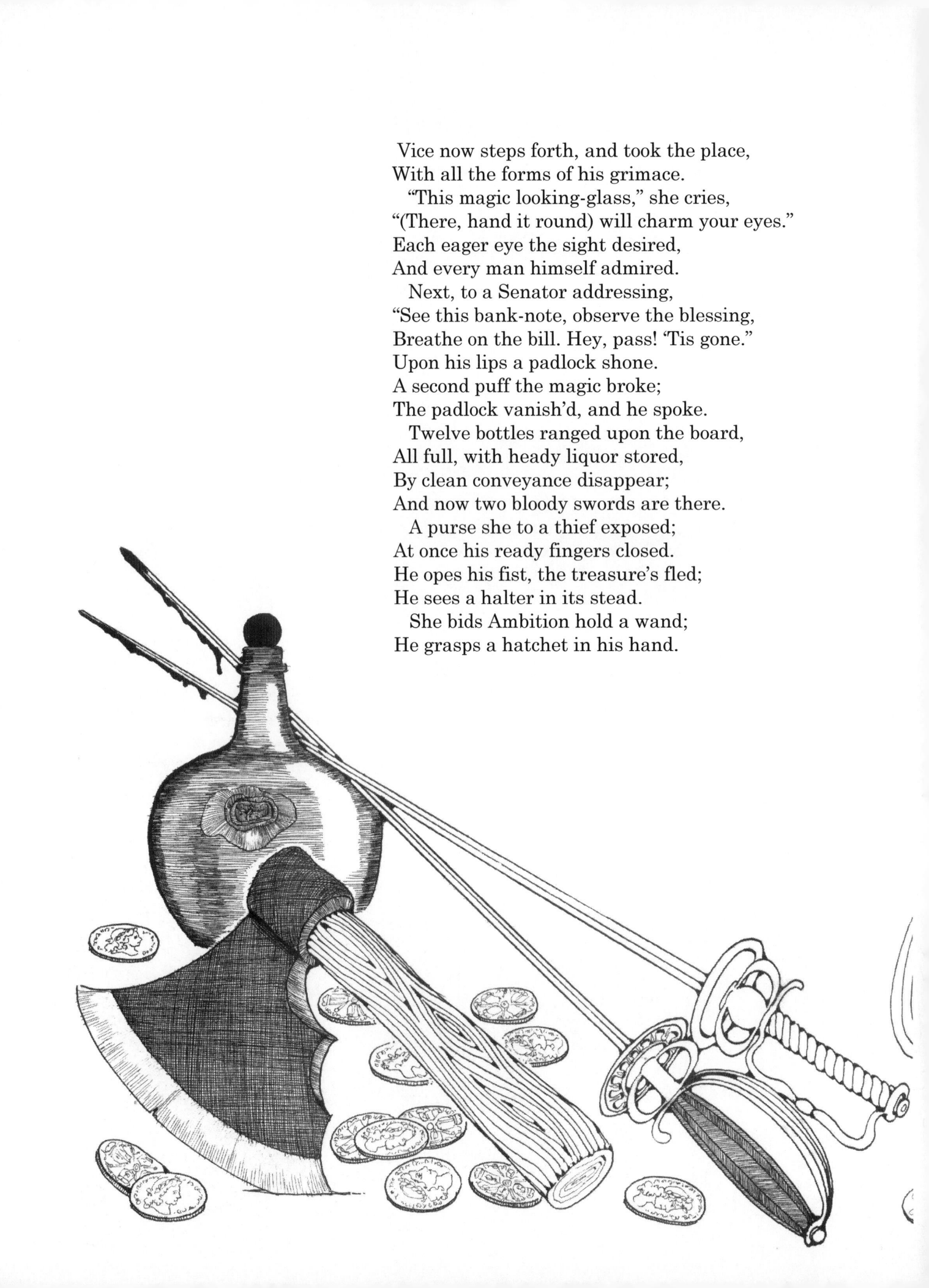

Vice now steps forth, and took the place,
With all the forms of his grimace.
　"This magic looking-glass," she cries,
"(There, hand it round) will charm your eyes."
Each eager eye the sight desired,
And every man himself admired.
　Next, to a Senator addressing,
"See this bank-note, observe the blessing,
Breathe on the bill. Hey, pass! 'Tis gone."
Upon his lips a padlock shone.
A second puff the magic broke;
The padlock vanish'd, and he spoke.
　Twelve bottles ranged upon the board,
All full, with heady liquor stored,
By clean conveyance disappear;
And now two bloody swords are there.
　A purse she to a thief exposed;
At once his ready fingers closed.
He opes his fist, the treasure's fled;
He sees a halter in its stead.
　She bids Ambition hold a wand;
He grasps a hatchet in his hand.

A box of charity she shows.
Blow here; and a churchwarden blows.
'Tis vanish'd with conveyance neat,
And on the table smokes a treat.
   She shakes the dice, the board she knocks,
And from all pockets fills her box.
   She next a meagre rake addrest:
"This picture see; her shape, her breast!
What youth, and what inviting eyes!
Hold her, and have her." With surprise,
His hand exposed a box of pills,
And a loud laugh proclaim'd his ills.
   A counter in a miser's hand,
Grew twenty guineas at command:
She bids his heir the sum retain,
And 'tis a counter now again.
   A guinea with her touch, you see
Take every shape but Charity;
And not one thing you saw, or drew,
But changed from what was first in view.
   The Juggler now, in grief of heart,
With this submission own'd her art.
"Can I such matchless sleight withstand:
How practice hath improved your hand!
But now and then I cheat the throng;
You every day, and all day long."

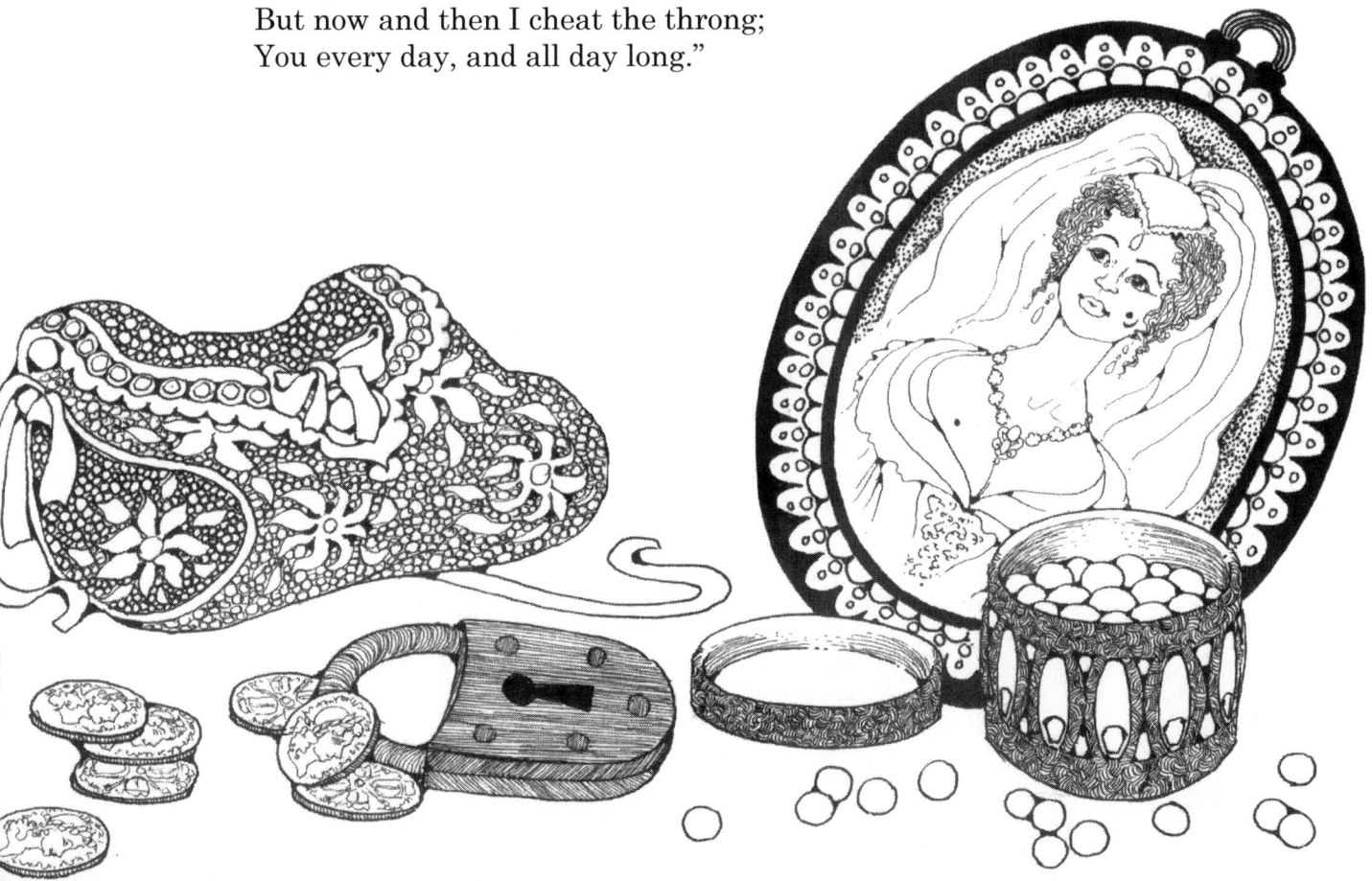

FABLE 43

The Council of Horses

Upon a time a neighing Steed,
Who grazed among a numerous breed,
With mutiny had fired the train,
And spread dissension through the plain.
On matters that concern'd the state
The Council met in grand debate.
A Colt, whose eyeballs flamed with ire
Elate with strength and youthful fire,
In haste stept forth before the rest,
And thus the listening throng addrest:
  "Good gods! how abject is our race,
Condemn'd to slavery and disgrace
Shall we our servitude retain,
Because our sires have borne the chain?
Consider, friends, your strength and might;
'Tis conquest to assert your right.
How cumbrous is the gilded coach!
The pride of man is our reproach.
Were we design'd for daily toil,
To drag the ploughshare through the soil,
To sweat in harness through the road,
To groan beneath the carrier's load?
How feeble are the two-legged kind!
What force is in our nerves combined!
Shall then our nobler jaws submit
To foam and champ the galling bit?
Shall haughty man my back bestride?
Shall the sharp spur provoke my side?
Forbid it heavens! Reject the rein;
Your shame, your infamy disdain.

Let him the lion first control,
And still the tiger's famish'd growl.
Let us, like them, our freedom claim,
And make him tremble at our name."
   A general nod approved the cause,
And all the circle neigh'd applause.
   When, lo! with grave and solemn pace,
A steed advanced before the race,
With age and long experience wise;
Around he cast his thoughtful eyes,
And, to the murmurs of the train,
Thus spoke the Nestor of the plain:
   "When I had health and strength, like you,
The toils of servitude I knew;
Now grateful man rewards my pains,
And gives me all these wide domains.
At will, I crop the year's increase;
My latter life is rest and peace.
I grant to man we lend our pains,
And aid him to correct the plains;
And doth not he divide the care,
Through all the labours of the year?
How many thousand structures rise,
To fence us from inclement skies
For us he bears the sultry day,
And stores up all our winter's hay;
He sows, he reaps the harvest's gain,
We share the toil, and share the grain.
Since every creature was decreed
To aid each other's mutual need,
Appease your discontented mind,
And act the part by Heaven assign'd."
The tumult ceased. The Colt submitted;
And, like his ancestors, was bitted.

FABLE 44

The Hound and the Huntsman

Impertinence at first is borne
With heedless slight, or smiles of scorn:
Teased into wrath, what patience bears
The noisy fool who perseveres?
   The morning wakes, the Huntsman sounds,
At once rush forth the joyful Hounds;
They seek the wood with eager pace,
Through bush, through brier, explore the chase.
Now scatter'd wide they try the plain,
And snuff the dewy turf in vain.
What care, what industry, what pains!
What universal silence reigns!
   Ringwood, a dog of little fame,
Young, pert, and ignorant of game,
At once displays his babbling throat;
The pack, regardless of the note,
Pursue the scent; with louder strain
He still persists to vex the train.
   The Huntsman to the clamour flies,
The smacking lash he smartly plies.
His ribs all welk'd, with howling tone
The puppy thus express'd his moan:
   "I know the music of my tongue
Long since the pack with envy stung.
What will not spite? these bitter smarts
I owe to my superior parts."
   "When Puppies prate," the Huntsman cried,
"They show both ignorance and pride:
Fools may our scorn, not envy, raise;
For envy is a kind of praise.
Had not thy forward noisy tongue

Proclaim'd thee always in the wrong,
Thou might'st have mingled with the rest,
And ne'er thy foolish nose confest:
But fools, to talking ever prone,
Are sure to make their follies known."

FABLE 45

The Poet and the Rose

I hate the man who builds his name
On ruins of another's fame:
Thus prudes, by characters o'erthrown,
Imagine that they raise their own;
Thus scribblers covetous of praise,
Think slander can transplant the bays.
Beauties and bards have equal pride,
With both all rivals are decried.
Who praises Lesbia's eyes and feature,
Must call her sister "awkward creature;"
For the kind flattery's sure to charm,
When we some other nymph disarm.
  As in the cool of early day
A Poet sought the sweets of May,
The garden's fragrant breath ascends,
And every stalk with odour bends.
A Rose he pluck'd: he gazed, admired,
Thus singing, as the Muse inspired:

"Go, Rose, my Chloe's bosom grace;
How happy should I prove,
Might I supply that envied place
With never-fading love!
There, Phoenix-like, beneath her eye,
 Involved in fragrance, burn and die!
"Know, hapless flower! that thou shalt find
 More fragrant Roses there:
 see thy withering head reclined
 With envy and despair!
One common fate we both must prove;
 You die with envy, I with love."
  "Spare your comparisons," replied
An angry Rose, who grew beside.
"Of all mankind you should not flout us;
What can a Poet do without us!
In every love-song Roses bloom,
We lend you colour and perfume.
Does it to Chloe's charms conduce,
To found her praise on our abuse?
Must we, to flatter her, be made
To wither, envy, pine, and fade?"

FABLE 46

The Cur, the Horse, and the Shepherd's Dog

The lad of all-sufficient merit,
With modesty ne'er damps his spirit;
Presuming on his own deserts,
On all alike his tongue exerts:
His noisy jokes at random throws,
And pertly spatters friends and foes.
In wit and war the bully race
Contribute to their own disgrace:
Too late the forward youth shall find
That jokes are sometimes paid in kind;
Or if they canker in the breast,
He makes a foe who makes a jest.

   A village Cur, of snappish race,
The pertest puppy of the place,
Imagined that his treble throat
Was blest with Music's sweetest note:
In the mid road he basking lay,
The yelping nuisance of the way;
For not a creature pass'd along
But had a sample of his song.

   Soon as the trotting Steed he hears,
He starts, he cocks his dapper ears;
Away he scours, assaults his hoof;
Now near him snarls, now barks aloof!
With shrill impertinence attends,
Nor leaves him till the village ends.
It chanced, upon his evil day,
A Pad came pacing down the way;
The Cur, with never ceasing tongue,
Upon the passing traveller sprung.
The Horse, from scorn provoked to ire,
Flung backward; rolling in the mire,
The Puppy howl'd, and bleeding lay;
The Pad in peace pursued his way.

   A Shepherd's Dog, who saw the deed,
Detesting the vexatious breed,

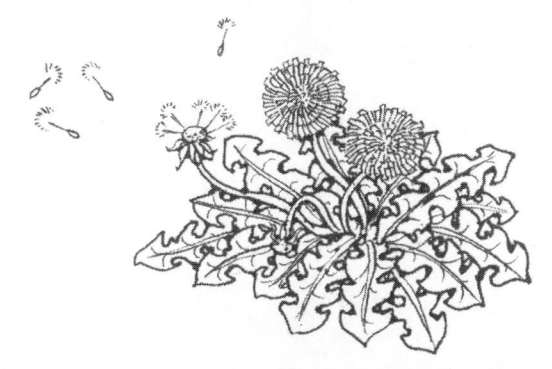

Bespoke him thus: "When coxcombs prate,
They kindle wrath, contempt, or hate;
Thy teasing tongue had judgment tied,
Thou hadst not, like a Puppy, died."

FABLE 47

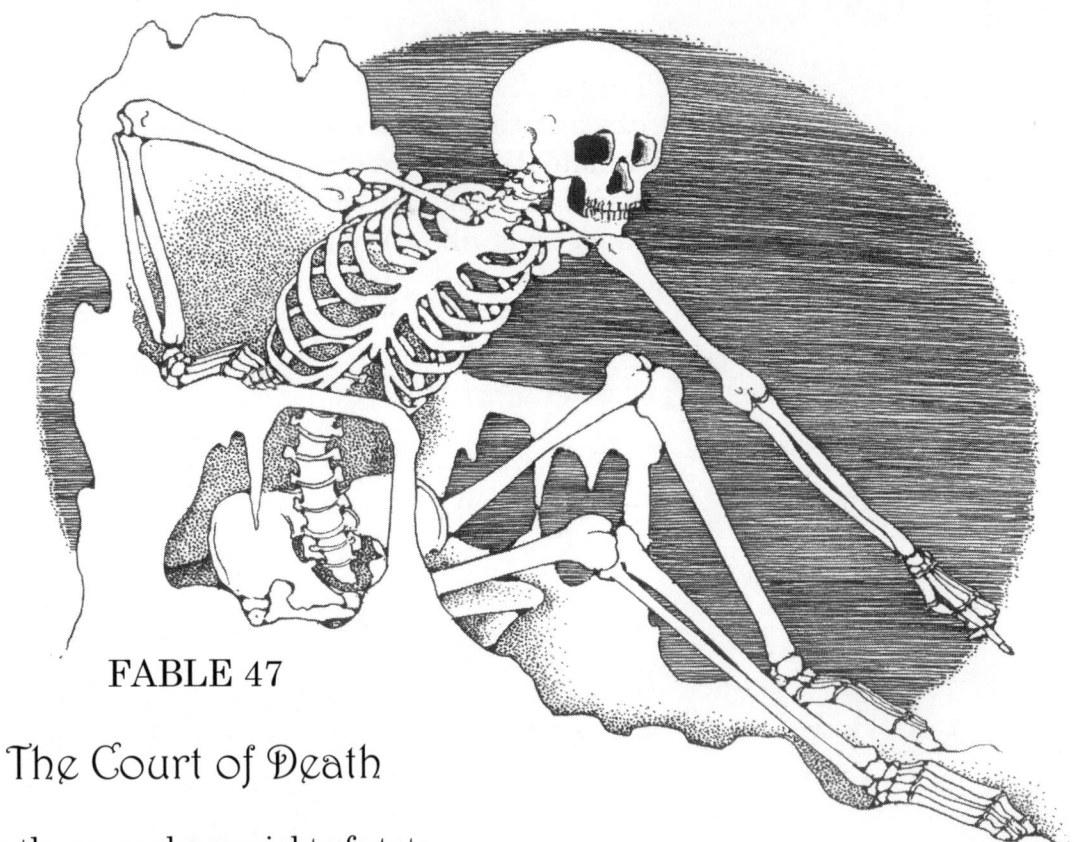

The Court of Death

Death, on a solemn night of state,
In all his pomp of terror sate:
Th' attendants of his gloomy reign,
Diseases dire, a ghastly train!
Crowd the vast court. With hollow tone,
A voice thus thunder'd from the throne:
"This night our minister we name;
Let every servant speak his claim;
Merit shall bear this ebon wand."
All, at the word, stretch'd forth their hand.
   Fever, with burning heat possess'd,
Advanced, and for the wand address'd:
   "I to the weekly bills appeal,
Let those express my fervent zeal;
On every slight occasion near,
With violence I persevere."
   Next Gout appears with limping pace,
Pleads how he shifts from place to place
From head to foot how swift he flies,
And every joint and sinew plies;
Still working when he seems suppress'd,
A most tenacious stubborn guest.
   A haggard Spectre from the crew
Crawls forth, and thus asserts his due:
"'Tis I who taint the sweetest joy,
And in the shape of Love destroy:
My shanks, sunk eyes, and noseless face,
Prove my pretension to the place."

Stone urg'd his ever-growing force;
And, next, Consumption's meagre corse,
With feeble voice, that scarce was heard,
Broke with short coughs, his suit preferr'd:
"Let none object my lingering way,
I gain, like Fabius, by delay;
Fatigue and weaken every foe
By long attack, secure, though slow."
Plague represents his rapid power,
Who thinn'd a nation in an hour.
All spoke their claim, and hoped the wand.
Now expectation hush'd the band,
When thus the Monarch from the throne:
   "Merit was ever modest known.
What, no Physician speak his right!
None here! but fees their toils requite.
Let then Intemperance take the wand,
Who fills with gold their zealous hand.
You, Fever, Gout, and all the rest,
(Whom wary men, as foes, detest)
Forego your claim; no more pretend;
Intemperance is esteem'd a friend.
He shares their mirth, their social joys,
And as a courted guest destroys:
The charge on him must justly fall,
Who finds employment for you all."

FABLE 48

The Gardener and the Hog

A Gardener of peculiar taste,
 On a young Hog his favour placed,
Who fed not with the common herd;
His tray was to the hall preferr'd:
He wallow'd underneath the board,
Or in his master's chamber snored,
Who fondly stroked him every day,
And taught him all the puppy's play.
Where'er he went, the grunting friend
Ne'er fail'd his pleasure to attend.
 As on a time the loving pair
Walk'd forth to tend the garden's care,
The master thus address'd the Swine:
 "My house, my garden, all is thine!
On turnips feast whene'er you please,
And riot in my beans and peas;
If the potato's taste delights,
Or the red carrot's sweet invites,
Indulge thy morn and evening hours,
But let due care regard my flowers:
My tulips are my garden's pride:
What vast expense those beds supplied:"

The Hog by chance one morning roam'd,
Where with new ale the vessels foam'd:
He munches now the steaming grains,
Now with full swill the liquor drains.
Intoxicating fumes arise:
He reels, he rolls his winking eyes:
Then staggering through the garden scours,
And treads down painted ranks of flowers:
With delving snout he turns the soil,
And cools his palate with the spoil.
The master came, the ruin spied;
   "Villain; suspend thy rage," he cried,
"Hast thou, thou most ungrateful sot,
My charge, my only charge, forgot?
What, all my flowers! "no more he said,
But gazed and sigh'd, and hung his head.
   The Hog, with stuttering speech returns:
"Explain, Sir, why your anger burns.
See there, untouch'd, your tulips strown,
For I devour'd the roots alone."
   At this the Gardener's passion grows;
From oaths and threats he fell to blows.
The stubborn brute the blow sustains,
Assaults his leg, and tears the veins.
   Ah! foolish Swain, too late you find
That sties were for such friends design'd!
Homeward he limps with painful pace,
Reflecting thus on past disgrace:
   "Who cherishes a brutal mate,
Shall mourn the folly soon or late."

FABLE 49

The Man and the Flea

Whether on earth, in air, or main,
Sure everything alive is vain!
   Does not the hawk all fowls survey,
As destined only for his prey?
And do not tyrants, prouder things,
Think men were born for slaves to kings?
   When the crab views the pearly strands,
Or Tagus, bright with golden sands;
Or crawls beside the coral grove,
And hears the ocean roll above;
"Nature is too profuse," says he,
"Who gave all these to pleasure me!"
   When bordering pinks and roses bloom,
And every garden breathes perfume
When peaches glow with sunny dyes,
Like Laura's cheek when blushes rise;
When the huge figs the branches bend,
When clusters from the vine depend,
The snail looks round on flower and tree,
And cries, "All these were made for me!"
   "What dignity's in human nature?"
Says Man, the most conceited creature,
As from a cliff he casts his eye,
And view'd the sea and arched sky.
The sun was sunk beneath the main;
The moon and all the starry train
Hung the vast vault of Heaven: the Man
His contemplation thus began:

"When I behold this glorious show,
And the wide watery world below,
The scaly people of the main,
The beasts that range the wood or plain,
The wing'd inhabitants of air,
The day, the night, the various year,
And know all these by Heaven design'd
As gifts to pleasure human kind,
I cannot raise my worth too high;
Of what vast consequence am I!"
"Not of th' importance you suppose,"
Replies a Flea upon his nose.
"Be humble, learn thyself to scan;
Know, pride was never made for man,
'Tis vanity that swells thy mind,
What, Heaven and earth for thee design'd!
For thee, made only for our need,
That more important Fleas might feed."

FABLE 50

The Hare and Many Friends

Friendship, like love, is but a name,
Unless to one, you stint the flame.
The child, whom many fathers share,
Hath seldom known a father's care.
'Tis thus in friendships; who depend
On many, rarely find a friend.
   A Hare who, in a civil way,
Complied with everything, like GAY,
Was known by all the bestial train
Who haunt the wood or graze the plain.
Her care was never to offend,
And every creature was her friend.
As forth she went, at early dawn,
To taste the dew-besprinkled lawn,
Behind, she hears the hunter's cries,
And from the deep mouth'd thunder, flies.
She starts, she stops, she pants for breath;
She hears the near advance of death;
She doubles to mislead the hound,
And measures back her mazy round;
Till, fainting in the public way,
Half dead with fear, she gasping lay.
   What transport in her bosom grew,
When first the Horse appear'd in view!
   "Let me," says she, "your back ascend,
And owe my safety to a friend.
You know my feet betray my flight;
To friendship every burden's light."
   The Horse replied, "Poor honest Puss,
It grieves my heart to see thee thus:
Be comforted, relief is near,
For all your friends are in the rear."

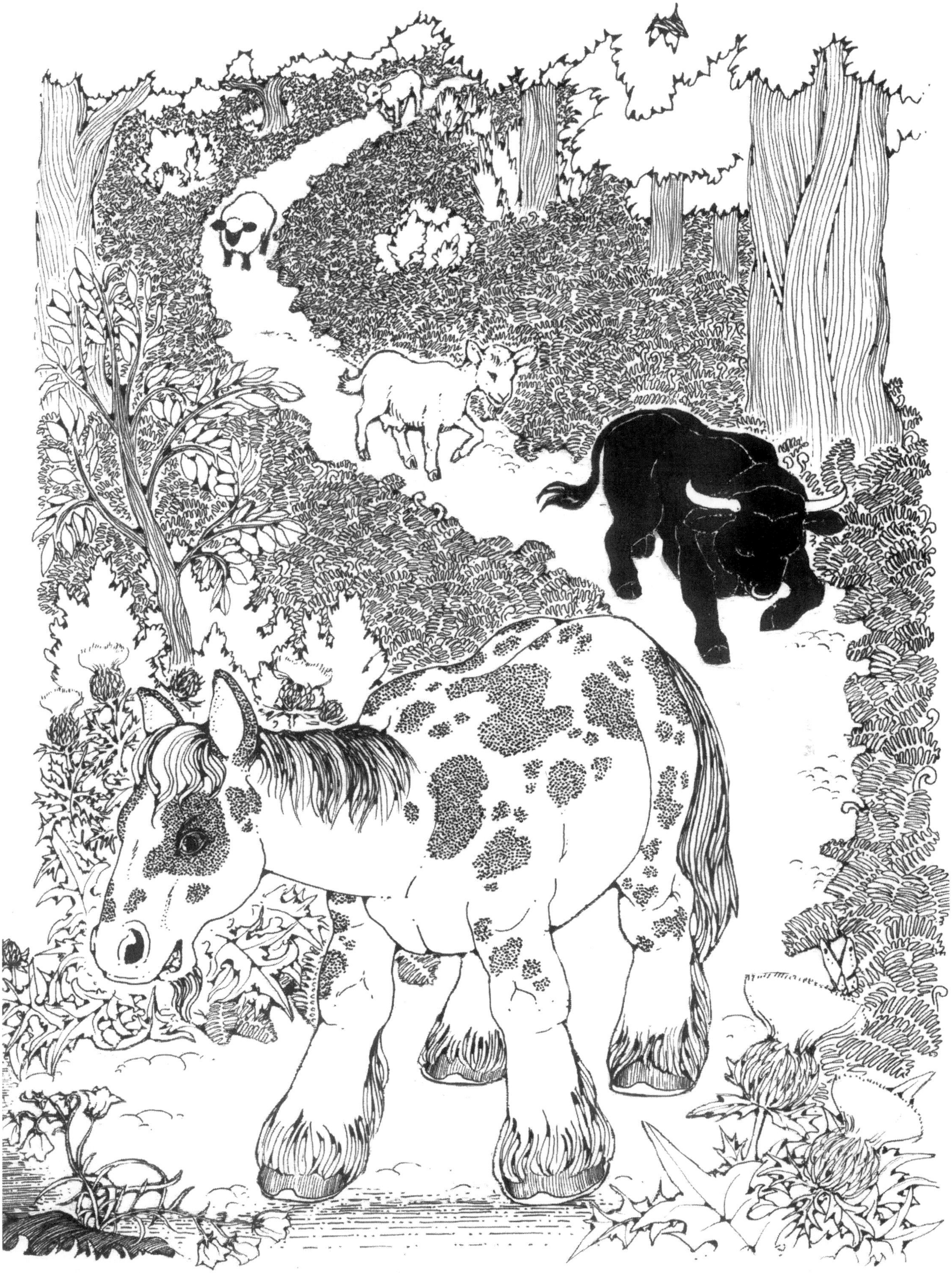

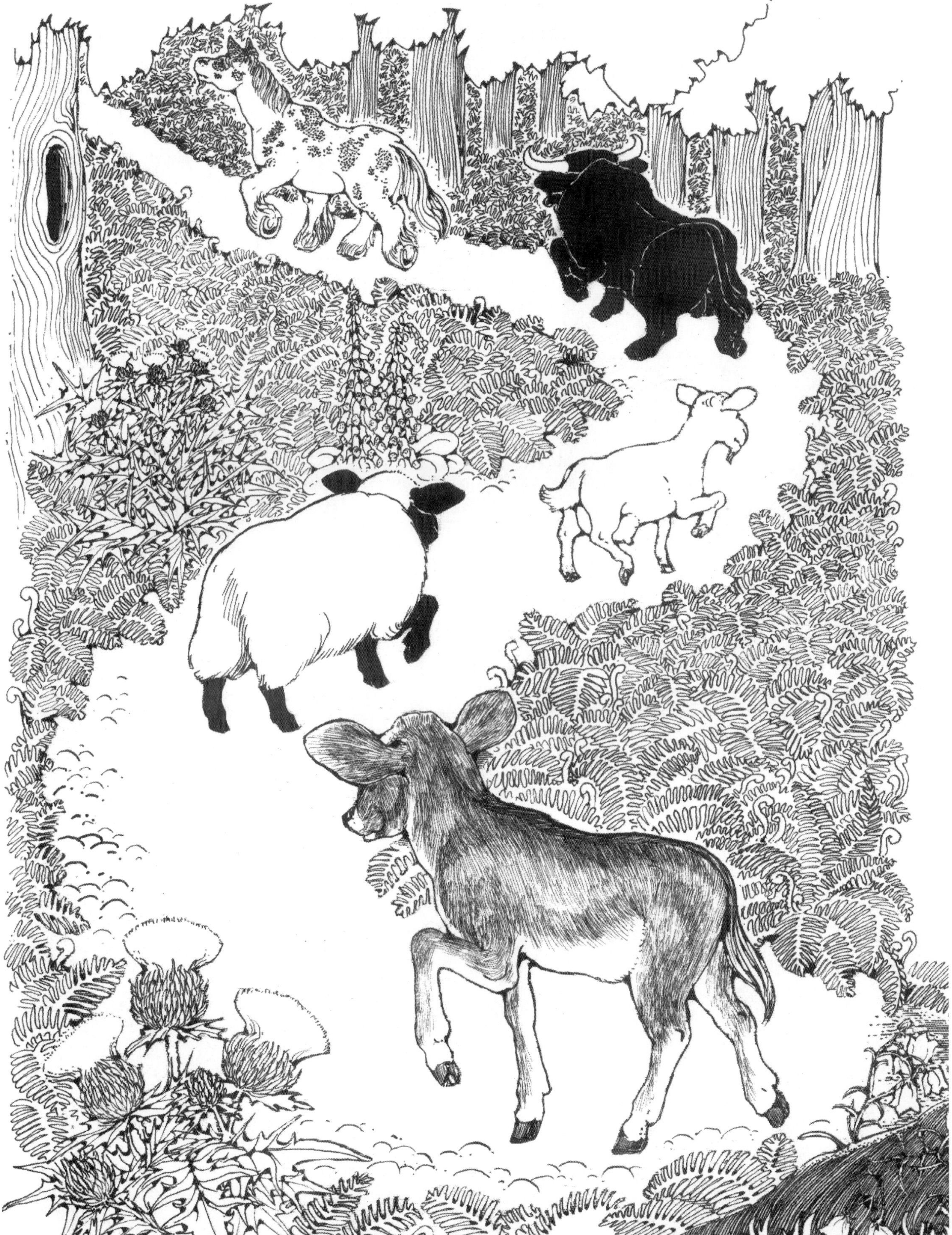

She next the stately Bull implored;
And thus replied the mighty lord:
"Since ev'ry beast alive can tell
That I sincerely wish you well,
I may, without offence, pretend
To take the freedom of a friend.
Love calls me hence; a favourite cow
Expects me near yon barley-mow;
And when a lady's in the case,
You know all other things give place.
To leave you thus might seem unkind,
But see, the Goat is just behind."
   The Goat remark'd her pulse was high,
Her languid head, her heavy eye:
"My back," says he, "may do you harm;
The Sheep's at hand, and wool is warm."
   The Sheep was feeble, and complain'd
His sides a load of wool sustain'd:
Said he was slow; confess'd his fears;
For hounds eat sheep as well as Hares.
She now the trotting Calf address'd,
To save from death a friend distress'd:
"Shall I," says he, "of tender age,
In this important care engage?
Older and abler pass'd you by;
How strong are those I how weak am I!
Should I presume to bear you hence,
Those friends of mine may take offence.
Excuse me, then: you know my heart;
But dearest friends, alas! must part.
How shall we all lament! Adieu,
For see, the hounds are just in view."

1685 ~ 1732